ATTP 3-39.32 (FM 3-19.30)

Physical Security

August 2010

Headquarters, Department of the Army

Army Tactics, Techniques, and Procedures
No. 3-39.32 (FM 3-19.30)

Headquarters
Department of the Army
Washington, DC, 3 August 2010

Physical Security

Contents

Distribution Restriction: Approved for public release; distribution is unlimited.

*This publication supersedes FM 3-19.30, 8 January 2001.

Figures

Tables

Preface

Army Tactics, Techniques, and Procedures (ATTP) 3-39.32 provides doctrinal guidance for personnel who are responsible for planning and executing physical security programs. It is the basic reference for training security personnel and is intended to be used in conjunction with the Army Regulation (AR) 190 series (Military Police), Security Engineering Unified Facilities Criteria (UFC) publications, Department of Defense (DOD) directives, and other Department of the Army (DA) publications. This publication applies to the Active Army, the Army National Guard (ARNG)/Army National Guard of the United States (ARNGUS), and the United States Army Reserves (USAR) unless otherwise stated.

Prevention and protection are the two primary concerns of physical security; both serve the security interests of people, equipment, and property. This ATTP establishes physical security as a supporting component of the protection warfighting function and describes defensive measures that enable protection tasks, such as operations security, antiterrorism, operational area security, survivability, and information protection.

Information concerning the Commander's Crime Prevention Program has been removed from this publication and will be included in the next revision of Field Manual (FM) 19-10 (to be renumbered ATTP 3-39.10). Information concerning crime prevention can also be obtained by contacting the United States Army Maneuver Support Center of Excellence (MSCoE), Concepts, Organization, and Doctrine Development Division, 320 MANSCEN Loop, Suite 270, Fort Leonard Wood, Missouri 65473-8929.

ATTP 3-39.32 is organized into 11 chapters and 6 appendixes, which provide additional details on selected physical security topics. A brief description of each chapter and appendix follows.

- Chapter 1, Physical Security Challenges, describes how the physical security program supports the principles of the protection warfighting function through the coordinated efforts of policies, plans, and procedures that are specifically designed to achieve a strong protection posture.
- Chapter 2, Physical Security Planning, describes how planning committees, such as the protection working group, play an integral part in the planning process. The chapter introduces the Army Military Police Security Management System countermeasures as the primary planner's tool for physical security surveys and inspections.
- Chapter 3, Site Design Approach, lays the foundation for initial security design planning considerations that are required for new construction, renovation, and temporary structures. The chapter discusses perimeter and internal security systems.
- Chapter 4, Protective Barriers, describes emplacement considerations of barriers and fencing (to form the perimeter of controlled areas) and passive and active vehicle barriers (to impede, channel, or stop vehicle traffic).
- Chapter 5, Security Lighting, provides the principles of security lighting and technical information for the minimum levels of illumination and lighting uniformity required for various applications.
- Chapter 6, Electronic Security System, describes the five major components of electronic security systems (ESSs) and provides technical data concerning electronic interior and exterior sensors and alarm systems.
- Chapter 7, Access Control Points, discusses the policies, technical guidance, and procedures used at Army access control points (ACPs). The chapter describes the four ACP zones and the procedures for vehicle inspection and hand-carried item examination.
- Chapter 8, Key Control and Locking Systems Security, describes the duties and responsibilities of the key custodian, describes procedures for key and lock control, and provides technical information on the various types of locking devices.
- Chapter 9, Security Forces, highlights the authority and jurisdiction of security forces, describes various types of security forces, and discusses the development of comprehensive security plans and orders.

- Chapter 10, Physical Security for In-Transit Forces, describes risk management for deploying forces and security procedures for in-port cargo and rail cargo protection.
- Chapter 11, Resource Management, lays out the foundation for documenting physical security resource requirements, conducting program and budget reviews, prioritizing requirements, and identifying funding sources.
- Appendix A, Sample Physical Security Plan, provides an example of a physical security plan and describes annexes required per AR 190-13.
- Appendix B, Selected Reachback Capabilities, highlights various official organizations and agencies that provide useful information to enhance situational awareness for commanders and physical security planners.
- Appendix C, Sample Physical Security Checklist, provides a guide for physical security personnel in developing checklists tailored to meet their specific needs.
- Appendix D, Bomb Threats, offers a sample bomb-threat data card and provides guidelines for bomb-threat planning, evacuation drills, and search considerations.
- Appendix E, Key Control Register and Inventory Form, shows a sample completed DA Form 5513 (Key Control Register and Inventory).
- Appendix F, Sample Key Control and Lock Security Checklist, provides an example to help physical security personnel develop a key control checklist that is specifically designed to meet their needs.

Terms that have joint or Army definitions are identified in both the glossary and the text. Glossary references: The glossary lists most terms used in ATTP 3-39.32 that have joint or Army definitions. Terms for which ATTP 3-39.32 is the proponent (the authority) are indicated with an asterisk in the glossary. Text references: Definitions for which ATTP 3-39.32 is the proponent are printed in boldface in the text. These terms and their definitions will be incorporated into the next revision of FM 1-02. For other definitions in the text, the term is italicized, and the number of the proponent follows the definition.

The proponent for this publication is the United States Army Training and Doctrine Command (TRADOC). Send comments and recommendations on DA Form 2028 (Recommended Changes to Publications and Blank Forms) directly to Commandant, United States Army Military Police School, ATTN: ATZT-CDC, 320 MANSCEN Loop, Suite 270, Fort Leonard Wood, Missouri 65473-8929. Submit an electronic DA Form 2028 or comments and recommendations in the DA Form 2028 format by email to <leon.cdidcodddmpdoc@conus.army.mil>.

Unless this publication states otherwise, masculine nouns and pronouns do not refer exclusively to men.

Introduction

Physical security **is that part of the Army security system, based on threat analysis, concerned with procedures and physical measures designed to safeguard personnel, property, and operations; to prevent unauthorized access to equipment, facilities, materiel, and information; and to protect against espionage, terrorism, sabotage, damage, misuse, and theft.** The security of property, equipment, facilities, and personnel is the responsibility of each military and civilian leader throughout DOD. Commanders protect personnel, information, and critical resources in all locations and situations against a wide spectrum of threats through the development and implementation of effective physical security programs, policies, and procedures.

The physical security program is the interrelationship of various components that complement each other to produce a comprehensive approach to security matters. These components include—at the minimum—the physical security plan, physical security inspections and surveys, participation in force protection working groups, and a continuing assessment of the installation's physical security posture. The physical security program resides with the installation provost marshal or director of emergency services who coordinates and implements the physical security functions as prescribed in AR 190-13.

Physical security measures and procedures support and enable many of the tasks that comprise the Army protection warfighting function (see FM 3-37 for more information). For example, physical security measures, as they pertain to antiterrorism, identify physical vulnerabilities to terrorist attacks of bases, personnel, and materiel; and take actions to reduce or eliminate those vulnerabilities. Survivability operations and general engineering support may be required to emplace compensatory measures for identified vulnerabilities. The physical security system builds on the premise that baseline security and the preparedness posture are based on the local threat, site-specific vulnerabilities, identified critical assets, and available resources.

While the basic principles of physical security are enduring, security technology, components, and analytical tools continue to evolve and improve. Today, commanders have a full array of sophisticated ESSs, sensitive chemical sensors, explosive detection devices, and forward-looking infrared (IR) radar systems to employ. These systems provide multilayered, 360-degree, real-time capability to detect, assess, alert, and act against air and ground threats at fixed sites. The goal of the security system for an installation, area, facility, or asset is to employ security in depth to preclude or reduce the potential for sabotage, theft, trespass, terrorism, espionage, or other criminal activity. In remote locations, commanders of expeditionary forces protect combat power by establishing a system of complementary, overlapping security measures to control access to critical resources and personnel. Where sophisticated ESSs are not practical, physical security measures such as physical barriers, clear zones, lighting, access and key control, the use of security badges, and defensive positions greatly enhance a unit's protective posture.

Recent improvements in analytical tools such as the United States Army Security Management System (Countermeasures) (SMS [CM]) have enhanced physical security surveys and inspection processes. This system enables commanders to quickly detect vulnerabilities that may be exploited by terrorists and criminals and to develop options that eliminate or mitigate those vulnerabilities.

The physical security policy is established by the AR 190 series, encompassing those functions that safeguard personnel, installations, critical resources, and information. The Office of the Provost Marshal General is the proponent for physical security and establishes policy and regulations pertaining to physical security operations.

This page intentionally left blank.

Chapter 1

Physical Security Challenges

Today, United States (U.S.) military forces face a significant threat from adversaries employing a variety of tactics, such as improvised explosive devices (IEDs), snipers, and indirect-fire weapons. Attacks are often complex and executed on multiple avenues of approach, using a combination of weapons and tactics. Commanders are increasingly challenged to protect personnel, installations, critical assets, information, and military operations against threats that range from traditional to irregular and from catastrophic to disruptive. The security challenge is partially influenced by the geographic location, size, type, jurisdiction, available assets, and mission of the facility, installation, or unit. A major contributing factor to the vulnerability of Army installations is the relatively fixed nature of operations. Adversaries can observe operational patterns and determine existing defensive measures. Such vulnerabilities can be reduced by developing proper standoff distances, installing early detection sensors and countersurveillance devices, aggressively patrolling with well-trained security forces, and implementing random antiterrorism measures (RAMs).

PHYSICAL SECURITY AND THE PROTECTION WARFIGHTING FUNCTION

1-1. The operational environment is a composite of the conditions, circumstances, and influences that affect the employment of capabilities and bear on the decisions of the commander. In every operational environment, there are potential hazards and threats that must be identified and mitigated. Hazards are conditions with the potential to cause injury, illness, or death to personnel; threats include an adversary's intent on damaging or destroying property and injuring or killing personnel.

1-2. Commanders differentiate hazards from threats and develop focused protection strategies and priorities that match protection capabilities. Physical security measures primarily focus on threat deterrence, detection, delay, and response.

1-3. *Protection* is the preservation of the effectiveness and survivability of mission-related military and nonmilitary personnel, equipment, facilities, information, and infrastructure deployed or located within or outside the boundaries of a given operational area (FM 3-37).

1-4. The Army's physical security program supports the forms and principles of protection through the coordinated efforts of policies, plans, and procedures that are specifically designed to achieve a strong physical security posture. Commanders apply physical security measures to the tasks and systems that influence and support protection. Together, these activities provide a coherent protection effort.

FORMS OF PROTECTION

1-5. Military operations recognize five forms of protection to achieve success—prevention, deterrence, passive defense, active security, and mitigation. They reflect the continuous nature of protection and provide a method to develop and employ protection capabilities (see FM 3-37). When properly applied, physical security measures can greatly influence each form of protection.

- **Prevention**. Commanders achieve prevention by planning and implementing security programs that are designed to prevent the effects of hazards and threats before they occur. Programs and activities such as antiterrorism, operations security, information operations, physical security, and crime prevention contribute to prevention efforts.

- **Deterrence**. Threats against personnel, resources, and installations can be greatly reduced when commanders establish robust security programs. Aggressive access control operations deter adversaries from attempting unauthorized entry to bases. Hardened fortifications and well-trained and -equipped security forces reduce the likelihood that a base will become a target, and they can cause adversaries to choose a less defended target.

- **Passive defense**. Physical security's greatest contribution to passive defense may be the use of active and passive barriers, electronic surveillance and intrusion detection devices, and automated identification systems. These security measures protect personnel, critical assets, and installations and typically form the first line of defense against threats.

- **Active security**. Commanders in all operational environments protect personnel, assets, and installations by maintaining a security force with the ability to detect, interdict, disrupt, and defeat hazards and threats. Even the most sophisticated ESS requires a well-trained, ready force to respond to, assess, and control the incident. Security personnel are the human responses to unauthorized acts, and they are trained to apply the appropriate level of force (lethal and nonlethal) to protect people, resources, information, and facilities.

- **Mitigation**. Mitigation consists of the activities and efforts that have the ability to minimize the consequences of attacks and designated emergencies on personnel, physical assets, and information. Commanders restore and safeguard forces through effective consequence management. Damage assessments, site security, personnel recovery, and decontamination contribute to restoration efforts. Together, these activities speed recovery and help the community return to normal operations.

PRINCIPLES OF PROTECTION

1-6. Successful protection is characterized by the integration of five principles—full dimension, layered, redundant, integrated, and enduring. These principles are not applied the same way in every situation, but provide commanders a context for planning protection efforts, developing protection strategies, and allocating resources (see FM 3-37). Not surprisingly, effective physical security measures parallel these principles and integrate many of the same qualities.

- **Full dimension.** Protection is continuous and asymmetrical; it considers threats and hazards in all directions, at all times, and in all environments. Likewise, security efforts must be designed to deter, detect, delay, and disrupt threats and hazards in all directions, at all times, in all environments.

- **Layered.** Protection capabilities are layered to provide strength and depth to the overall protection system and reduce the effects of a hazard or threat. Physical security efforts emphasize the concept of defense in depth by placing the asset to be protected in the innermost ring of security. The layers of security are provided at increasing distances from the protected asset. The number of layers, the components that comprise them, and their resistance to penetration depend on the threat and the importance of the asset to be protected.

- **Redundant.** Redundancy ensures that critical activities, systems, and capabilities have a secondary or backup system of equal or greater capability. Protection efforts are often redundant and overlapping anywhere that vulnerability, weakness, or failure is identified or expected. Security measures are often planned in the same manner with backup capabilities. For example, restricted facilities are typically augmented by alarm systems with assessment capabilities and physically checked by trained security personnel. ACPs often employ obstacles, active and passive barriers, vehicle-arresting systems, and final denial barriers to control, stop, and defeat a threat vehicle.

- **Integrated.** Protection is integrated with all other activities, systems, efforts, and capabilities that are associated with military operations to provide strength and structure to the overall protection effort. Security planning takes into account the systems, plans, and resources from all tenant and civilian agencies. When a capability is lacking, commanders establish memorandums of agreement with local or host nation (HN) agencies to fill security gaps and integrate existing resources.

- **Enduring.** Protection has an enduring quality that differentiates it from the conduct of defense or specific security operations. Physical security efforts are continuous, and some security measures are more enduring than others. The degrees of protection may increase or decrease, depending on the current threat assessment. However, security personnel and resources must be able to maintain a reasonable level of protection for extended periods.

PROTECTION TASKS AND SYSTEMS

1-7.   The protection warfighting function serves to focus protection efforts on 12 specific tasks or systems that help protect personnel, assets, and information:

- Air missile defense.
- Personnel recovery.
- Fratricide avoidance.
- Force health protection.
- Chemical, biological, radiological, and nuclear operations.
- Safety.
- Explosive ordnance disposal.
- Operations security.
- Antiterrorism.
- Operational area security.
- Survivability.
- Information protection.

1-8.   Physical security policies, procedures, and systems are nested in, and support, several key tasks of protection, including operations security, antiterrorism, operational area security, survivability, and information protection.

OPERATIONS SECURITY

1-9.   *Operations security* is a process of identifying essential elements of friendly information and subsequently analyzing friendly actions attendant to military operations and other activities to identify those actions that can be observed by adversary intelligence systems, determine indicators hostile intelligence systems might obtain that could be interpreted or pieced together to derive critical information in time to be useful to adversaries, and select and execute measures that eliminate or reduce to an acceptable level the vulnerabilities of friendly actions to adversary exploitation. (FM 3-13)

1-10. Operations security is one of the core elements of information operations, and physical security is a supporting element (see AR 530-1). Physical security enhances operations security by providing physical measures that are designed to—

- Safeguard personnel.
- Prevent unauthorized access to information, equipment, installations, material, and documents.
- Safeguard against espionage, sabotage, damage, and theft.

ANTITERRORISM

1-11. Antiterrorism is the Army's defensive program to protect against terrorism. Effective antiterrorism programs synchronize intelligence, composite risk management, and existing security programs to provide a holistic approach to defend against terrorist threats.

1-12. The physical security officers (PSOs) provide assistance in the defensive planning, implementation, and control for antiterrorism operations. They provide expert advice and assistance in developing crime prevention programs and physical security plans and programs—which help identify, reduce, or eliminate conditions that are favorable to criminal, terrorist, and insurgent activities.

1-13. Commanders rely on the PSO to conduct the comprehensive evaluation of units, facilities, and installations to determine the preparedness to deter, withstand, and recover from the full range of adversarial capabilities based on the threat assessment, crime and criminal threat analysis, compliance with protection standards, and risk management.

1-14. Crime and criminal threat analysis is a continuous process of compiling and examining available information concerning potential criminal threat activities. Criminal and terrorist groups or individuals may target U.S. military installations, personnel, or facilities. A criminal threat analysis reviews the factors of a threat group's operational capability, intentions, and activities, and is an essential step in identifying the threat posed by specific groups or individuals.

Note. Crime threat analysis techniques are described in FM 3-19.50.

1-15. Physical security systems installed in and around installations, facilities, and units form the physical backbone of antiterrorism efforts. The facilities, equipment, and personnel that form the installation security force are critical resources that help defend against terrorist attacks.

1-16. Physical security personnel, equipment, procedures, or devices used to protect security interests from possible threats include—

- DA police/security guards.
- Military working dogs (MWDs).
- Physical barriers.
- Badging systems.
- Secure containers.
- Locking devices.
- Intrusion-detection systems (IDSs).
- Security lighting.
- Electronic surveillance systems.
- Access control devices.
- Facility hardening.

OPERATIONAL AREA SECURITY

1-17. Operational area security is a form of active security operations conducted to protect friendly forces, installations, routes, and actions within an area of operations. Designated security forces (such as military police) saturate an area or position on key terrain to provide protection through early warning, reconnaissance, or surveillance, and guard against unexpected enemy attacks.

Note. FM 3-90 describes the tactics, techniques, and procedures for base defense, perimeter defense, and area security operations.

1-18. Area security efforts take advantage of the local security measures performed by units, regardless of their location in the area of operations. Physical security measures (such as access control operations) protect installations, facilities, and units from unauthorized access. Physical security plans, programs, and procedures are specifically designed to protect restricted areas. A **restricted area is any area to which entry is subject to special restrictions or control for security reasons or to safeguard property or material**. Security personnel patrol the installation or facility and respond to unauthorized acts, conduct security checks of restricted areas, and investigate suspicious activity.

SURVIVABILITY

1-19. Survivability includes all aspects of protecting personnel, weapons, and resources. Physical security efforts contribute to survivability operations by providing an integrated and multilayered defense in depth. Engineers install perimeter barriers—such as preformed concrete barriers, wire, and fencing material—that are designed to prevent unauthorized intrusions into fixed sites. Perimeter security efforts, such as intrusion detection and electronic surveillance, provide early warning and alert security forces of unauthorized attempts to enter controlled areas. Barrier plans are developed to block high-speed avenues of approach to high-risk targets. Access control systems (ACSs) such as cargo X-ray systems, explosive detection devices, and chemical sensors reduce vulnerabilities to explosives and chemical hazards.

INFORMATION PROTECTION

1-20. Information protection includes active or passive measures that protect and defend friendly information and information systems to ensure timely, accurate, and relevant friendly information protection.

1-21. The threat to automated information systems and information systems security involves deliberate, overt, and covert acts. This includes the physical threat to tangible property, such as the theft or destruction of computer hardware and communications systems. Also included is the threat of electronic, electromagnetic pulse, radio frequency (RF), or computer-based attacks on the information or communications components that control or make up critical Army command and control infrastructures. In most cases, the threat's target is the information itself rather than the system that transmits it.

1-22. Data links used to communicate sensitive information must be protected from compromise. Attempts to defeat the security system may range from simple efforts to cut or short the transmission line to more sophisticated attempts, such as tapping and substituting bogus signals. Data links are made more secure by physical protection, tamper protection, line supervision, and encryption.

1-23. As one of the critical supporting activities of information protection, physical security prevents unauthorized physical access to personnel, equipment, installations, materiel, and documents. Physical security supporting tasks include—

- Protecting operations plans and orders.
- Conducting physical security surveys and inspections.
- Restricting access through access control efforts.
- Ensuring that products do not contain classified information.
- Ensuring that classified information is properly protected.
- Documenting accountability and control.
- Safeguarding equipment that is used in electronic warfare, such as computers and computer components and cables.
- Enforcing the use of smart cards and common access cards.
- Designing strategies to keep aggressors away from areas where secure conversations are held.

1-24. Effective physical security ensures the availability of information systems used to conduct operations. It is based on—

- Identifying mission-essential information systems.
- Determining applicable risks and threat levels.
- Establishing relative security standards and using available resources to achieve the required level of physical security.
- Determining applicable protection measures.
- Coordinating with higher and adjacent units and HN agencies.
- Developing contingency plans for natural disasters, terrorist actions, or weapons of mass destruction attacks.

1-25. Commanders conduct physical security operations to safeguard resources, including information and information systems. Properly integrated, physical security complements the other information operations elements.

1-26. Physical security resources include—

- **Physical security programs**. Commanders establish physical security programs that are appropriate to their command's mission.
- **Physical security specialists**. Physical security specialists assigned to the provost marshal staff, or designated security office staff, identify vulnerable areas and recommend appropriate countermeasures. They also provide assessments of unit physical security measures.

1-27. The assistant chief of staff, information engagement (G-7), synchronizes physical security measures with other information protection efforts. First-line leaders ensure that Soldiers know regulatory requirements, understand how physical security measures protect information and information systems, and learn to recognize potential problem areas in physical and information security. Physical security plans encompassing the security of information systems should be coordinated with, or reviewed by, the unit information assurance officer.

PHYSICAL SECURITY OFFICER

1-28. The installation commander appoints, in writing, an installation PSO who reports through channels to the commander or deputy commander on all matters related to physical security (see AR 190-13). The provost marshal may serve as the PSO staff member of the division or corps protection cell.

1-29. The PSO coordinates installation physical security activities and supports tenant unit commanders with security requirements or enhancements beyond the unit's means. The installation PSO may be responsible for all or some of the following activities:

- Assessing installation physical security needs through inspections and surveys.
- Serving as the single point of contact for installation physical security equipment.
- Facilitating the physical security council.
- Advising the protection working group, antiterrorism working group, and planning teams on security-related matters.
- Conducting liaison with federal, state, local, and HN law enforcement agencies and uniformed Service intelligence agencies.
- Coordinating with engineers during the planning, design, and construction of new construction and renovation projects to identify physical security and antiterrorism requirements.

1-30. The training requirements for the PSO include a wide range of knowledge and skills. Formal training in conventional physical security, antiterrorism, and various police intelligence and advanced law enforcement courses is available at the United States Army Military Police School (USAMPS), Fort Leonard Wood, Missouri. In addition to security and law enforcement skills, the PSO should be thoroughly knowledgeable in all aspects of threat assessment and risk analysis. The results of these processes are the basis for planning physical security programs.

1-31. The PSO or physical security inspector conducts risk analysis for assets of all assigned units and activities, maintaining particular categories of Army assets described in AR 190-51 and other assets designated as mission essential by AR 190-13. Risk analysis is also conducted for the assets of units and activities before they occupy new or renovated facilities. The PSO normally performs risk analysis for assets to be located in new facilities during the planning stage of the new construction or renovation so that security measures can be incorporated at the project's inception.

1-32. Understanding the basic principles of security engineering is important for the PSO to ensure that security needs are addressed during the initial planning and design of facilities, ACPs, and controlled areas where there is a need for physical security systems. The security series of the UFC manuals provide detailed information on security requirements for new construction and renovation projects. Security engineering UFCs are discussed throughout this manual.

Chapter 2

Physical Security Planning

The approach to developing protective measures for assets is based on a systematic process that results in an integrated protective system. All Army assets at all locations do not require the same degree of protection. Physical security planning for installations and facilities is primarily a staff function that should include antiterrorism, intelligence, operations, security, logistics, engineers, budget personnel, and the facility user. Physical security planning may be a function of the protection working group or as part of a specific physical security council. Normally, the designated provost marshal or PSO recommends to the commander those installation activities that require special physical security considerations based on their mission-essential or critical status and vulnerability to hostile threats. The provost marshal or PSO is typically the focal point for the development of the installation physical security plan. Commanders of host or tenant activities are responsible for security planning within their activities (see AR 190-13).

PLANNING PROCESS

2-1. The physical security plan considers mobilization, war, and contingency operations. The plan is tied to the force protection condition (FPCON) and RAMs and should include provisions for increasing the physical security measures and procedures during periods of increased threat from terrorist or criminal elements or natural emergencies (see AR 190-13). Physical security planning should include the initial security measures and the consideration of security measures that are appropriate for longer timelines, even though such measures may not be implemented for months or years.

Note. Appendix A provides a sample physical security plan format.

2-2. Physical security planning includes coordinating physical security with operations security, law enforcement, information security, personnel security, communications security, automated information security, and counterintelligence and antiterrorism programs to provide an integrated and coherent effort (see DOD 5200.08-R).

2-3. Planning security measures may require the consideration of other more stringent requirements, such as explosive safety, legal or political considerations, historic preservation, and environmental concerns. Regulatory requirements for security must be coordinated with other agencies that may specify different levels of protection or impose specific restrictions.

PLAN DEVELOPMENT

2-4. When developing the physical security plan, close coordination and liaison should be effected between the military commander and adjacent installations and units; federal, state, and local agencies; and appropriate HN agencies.

2-5. The goal of the plan is to provide protection for personnel, facilities, and equipment within Army responsibility. The physical security plan is a living document that is designed to allow for increases in protection to facilitate changes in FPCON. The plan must include the provisions of AR 190-13, including contingency planning, access and exit controls, road closure procedures, and restriction of movement in specific areas designated by the commander. At the minimum, the plan should include special and general guard orders; protective barriers; and lighting, locking, and IDSs (see appendix A).

2-6. A vulnerability assessment is conducted to determine protection measures and develop physical security plans. This assessment is a systematic approach to identifying vulnerabilities of mission-essential assets, facilities, resources, and personnel. A mission-essential or vulnerable area (MEVA) is a facility or activity that, by virtue of its function, is evaluated by the commander as vital to the successful mission accomplishment. MEVAs may include information, equipment, property, and facilities. A facility or area should be designated as a MEVA if it is essential to mission accomplishment and vulnerable to a threat that is intent on destroying, damaging, taking, or tampering with property or equipment.

2-7. MEVAs are normally recommended by the provost marshal or the PSO and approved by the commander. Once approved, MEVAs are designated in writing and included in the installation physical security plan. A vulnerability assessment is conducted to prioritize and rank each MEVA for resource allocation.

Note. AR 190-13 provides a list of activities that should be considered for designation as a MEVA.

VULNERABILITY ASSESSMENT

2-8. Vulnerability assessments are part of an overall risk management process, which includes—

- Conducting a mission analysis to determine the assets, facilities, and personnel that need protection.
- Analyzing threat tactics.
- Determining asset vulnerabilities to threat tactics.
- Conducting risk analysis of each critical asset's vulnerability to determine the level of risk.
- Analyzing courses of action to mitigate or resolve vulnerabilities.
- Applying resources to mitigate or resolve vulnerabilities.

2-9. Vulnerability assessments should be conducted when—

- A unit, organization, or activity is activated.
- A new facility or area is occupied.
- No record exists of a prior vulnerability assessment.
- Significant changes or modifications to the unit/organization or facilities have occurred since the last assessment—changes such as construction or the renovation or loss of a security system that may impact the security posture.
- Significant changes are made to the security force.
- The commander determines that greater frequency is required.

2-10. Vulnerability assessments should be formally reviewed by the commander annually. The results of the annual review or update should be documented and forwarded through command channels to the appropriate higher headquarters for review.

2-11. The commander may use the protection working group to conduct the vulnerability assessments (see FM 3-37). Physical security surveys and inspections conducted in the previous 12-month period should be used during the assessment.

2-12. The following is the recommended format used to document the results of a vulnerability assessment. The documentation should include, at the minimum, the following information:

- The primary mission of the unit or organization.
- The commander's intent, including how the unit/organization mission supports the mission of the next higher headquarters.
- A description of the mission of each subordinate unit/organization.
- Information concerning critical assets.
  - Describe what assets are critical to the unit/organization mission and why.
  - Describe the risk level for each critical asset (see DA Pamphlet [Pam] 190-51).

- Describe the levels of protection for vehicle bombs (low, medium, and high) for each critical asset (see UFC 4-020-01).
- Describe the impact on the mission if a critical asset is lost or not available, and rank-order critical assets from most to least important.
- Provide a site description and surrounding areas, including maps and photographs, if available.
- Review functional schematics and engineering drawings for critical assets, equipment, and structures, and include any relevant information.
- Detailed threat and threat capability information.
  - Describe the spectrum of viable threats to the mission, facilities, assets, and personnel.
  - Describe the capabilities of each threat and how that capability applies to each critical asset. At the minimum, use the Army's annual threat assessment and the local threat statement.
  - Identify each potential threat to each critical asset. Address what specific threats apply to each asset as identified by the annual threat assessment or local threat statements. Be specific in stating likely threat objectives; threat tactics; capabilities; and tools, explosives, and weapons that the threat could use in the execution of their attack (see DA Pam 190-51).
  - Describe what threats were considered and eliminated, and why. Consider, at the minimum, insider adversaries, outsider adversaries, insider and outsider collusion, airborne attack, and natural or manmade disasters that compromise asset security and may make a critical asset vulnerable.
- A facility and asset tour, including a tour of the MEVA or critical asset and surrounding areas, to become knowledgeable of the site configuration, terrain, storage structures, security system, security forces, and technical operational activities at the asset. Note the logical avenues of approach, areas providing concealment, fields of fire into the asset, standoff distances, and likely points of attack. During the tour, the team should identify specific vulnerabilities from external and internal threats by—
  - Observing day and night operations.
  - Interviewing personnel.
  - Having security equipment and procedures demonstrated.
  - Noting how the security systems are used, including security forces and backup forces.
  - Asking "what-if" questions with reference to the possibility of covert or overt acts by insiders.
  - Concentrating on means to bypass, subvert, overwhelm, or interrupt elements in the security systems.
- Characterization of security systems, processes, policies, and procedures.
  - Describe the plans, policies, standing operating procedures (SOPs), physical protection, access control, and multielement protection measures that are in place to protect target locations from the threat spectrum. Characterization should be specific to all protection in place, relative to MEVAs and critical assets.
  - Describe the layers of protection, and include the condition of security components.
  - Describe the general condition of security components (vehicle barriers, entry gates, fences, access controls, locks, area lighting, alarms, communications equipment, protective equipment).

2-13. Other critical information that should be reported during the vulnerability assessment includes—

- **Security force status.** Describe the composition of security forces, including authorized and required strengths since the last review.
- **Potential targets.** Based on the mission, commander's intent, results of the asset criticality assessment, the threat, and threat capabilities, describe potential adversarial acts (sabotage, theft, loss, seizure, unauthorized access, use, and diversion) for each critical asset as a potential target.
- **Scenario development.** Describe, in detail, plausible threat scenarios that were developed for each potential target. Scenario development should use a two-party, adversary (red team) and defender (blue team) gaming approach. Each team develops a plan for attack and defense

independently. After the team conducts planning, the blue and red teams conduct a tabletop exercise to react to attacks and work out defense specifics of the protected facility. A neutral party observes and provides guidance on how to develop the defensive plan based on the red team's attack concept. Each team identifies asset vulnerabilities; selects what the team considers to be credible courses of actions that an adversary might use; and conveys responses by the security system to deter, detect, defend, and defeat an adversary.

- **Exercise results.** Describe the results of test exercises for each identified threat. For example, if an insider threat has been identified as a threat to the asset, conduct an exercise to determine its viability. Provide a recapitulation of security system probabilities, delay times for structures and barriers, adversary target task times, security force response times, and security force neutralization times. Determine—
  - If the response force responds within the appropriate time limits.
  - If in-place security systems mitigate the potential threat to an acceptable level.
  - What additional measures are required to mitigate the potential threat to an acceptable level.
- **Conclusions, vulnerabilities, and recommendations.** State the conclusions and recommendations that were developed during the assessment. Conclusions should express results that follow the vulnerability assessment. Recommendations should support conclusions and be designed to reduce the likelihood of success for identified vulnerabilities.
- **Commander's formal decision on conclusions and recommendations.** The commander should make a formal decision on the assessment team's conclusions and recommendations. Each identified vulnerability and recommended corrective action should be addressed as follows:
  - Conclusions/vulnerabilities.
  - Recommendations.
  - Commander's concurrence/nonconcurrence (with comment).
  - Corrective actions taken or planned or the commander's acceptance of risk.
- **Vulnerability assessment.** The vulnerability assessment documentation should be forwarded through command channels to the Army command. Each commander in the chain of command should review and endorse the vulnerability assessment documentation to ensure that appropriate corrective actions are initiated or accomplished.

2-14. Within 30 days of the visit, a summary narrative report and an annotated briefing should be delivered to the installation commander. Follow-on assistance for the commander may be applicable for improvement options, cost estimates, and generic sources of materials and equipment.

SECURITY MANAGEMENT SYSTEM (COUNTERMEASURES)

2-15. The SMS (CM) is used by all Army physical security personnel and planners to standardize the procedures used to conduct physical security inspections, surveys, planning, and programming. The system is a planning tool that presents a coherent view of the physical security posture for defined areas of responsibility. It provides a standardized set of risk analysis measurements that are based on risk management techniques as published by the National Institute of Standards and Technology. The SMS (CM) performs cost benefit analysis; allows the detailed scrutiny of threats, vulnerability, and loss expectancy; and standardizes the execution of physical security business processes. Applicable regulations and specific inspection criteria are embedded into the system, and it is capable of hosting datasets for multiple security domains. Key features include the following:

- Identifies assets and their value.
- Calculates vulnerabilities.
- Evaluates risk based on applicable threats.
- Facilitates the analysis of improvements to security posture.
- Determines compliance with rules and policies.
- Recommends corrective actions.
- Calculates anticipated losses.
- Performs cost-benefit analysis and return on investment calculations.

2-16. The SMS (CM) is used to schedule, conduct, and record physical security surveys and inspections; submit timely information to higher headquarters; justify program requirements; and create risk-mitigation action plans—based on trend analysis, cost/benefit analysis, and loss expectancy analysis as the means to determine best use of resources.

> *Note.* Additional information about the SMS (CM) can be found at Army Knowledge Online, <http://www.us.army.mil/suite/page/441649>.

PHYSICAL SECURITY SURVEY

2-17. A *physical security survey* **is a formal recorded assessment of an installation's overall physical security program, including electronic security measures**. The survey provides the commander with an assessment of the overall security posture in view of the threat and mission and informs the commander about the installation's physical security strengths and weaknesses.

2-18. Physical security surveys are encouraged, but not required, for stand-alone facilities if a physical security inspection provides the commander with the information necessary to determine the physical security posture of the facility—not just the tenant units. For example, an Armed Forces Reserve Center managed by the USAR might not require a survey if the center is assessed by conducting an inspection for each unit, including the landlord unit, shared space (such as a motor pool), and the property perimeter. The landlord normally makes the final determination concerning physical security surveys for stand-alone facilities.

2-19. Surveys are recorded and results analyzed using the SMS (CM). DA Form 2806-R (Physical Security Survey Report [LRA]) may be used if the SMS (CM) is not available. Survey reports should show findings of policy deficiencies, along with observations concerning the potential means to improve site security. Procedures and measures to evaluate include—

- Threat assessment procedures.
- Security forces, including types, availability, training, equipment, and guard orders.
- Compliance with access control procedures.
- Control of visitors and hand-carried items.
- Use of physical security equipment.
- Security lighting.
- Control, issuance, and accountability of keys used at the installation perimeter—for example, at limited access gates.
- Identification of critical areas and facilities.
- Process used to track physical security work orders and vulnerability mitigation efforts.
- Waivers and exceptions to policy.

2-20. Physical security surveys should be conducted every 36 months, when an installation is activated, and when no record exists of a previous survey. Sites with conventional arms, ammunition, and explosives (AA&E) bulk storage (see AR 190-11) or surety assets require a survey every 24 months. Any facility may be surveyed more frequently if the commander determines that greater frequency is required. Surveys should include—

- Executive summary.
- Detailed assessment of the installation's security posture.
- Recommended application of resources in a prioritized manner for the reduction of vulnerabilities.
- Exhibits (such as photographs, sketches, graphs, and charts) to clarify findings and recommendations.

2-21. A copy of the physical security survey (with exhibits) should be provided to the installation commander, Army command, direct reporting unit, or ARNG chain of command for information and additional action. A copy should also be provided to the Army Service Component Command of the appropriate combatant command.

2-22. A commander's report of corrective action taken should be submitted in response to the survey if policy deficiencies—not observations—were found. A copy of the report is furnished to the provost marshal/director of emergency services and retained until the next survey is completed.

2-23. A formal process should be followed to ensure that policy discrepancies are corrected. After corrective actions are taken, the physical security posture is reassessed based on the—

- Mission.
- Potential threat.
- Findings of the survey team.
- Comparison of findings from previous surveys and inspections.
- Areas considered overprotected or underprotected.

2-24. The physical security survey should be used to form the physical security resource plan, recommend allocation priorities and revisions to existing measures and procedures, or develop new measures and procedures. The highest priority should be given to activities that are considered essential to mission accomplishment.

PHYSICAL SECURITY INSPECTION

2-25. A *physical security inspection* **is a formal, recorded assessment of the physical protective measures and security procedures that are implemented to protect unit and activity assets.** The SMS (CM) is used to gather and record inspection information; DA Form 2806-1-R (Physical Security Inspection Report [LRA]) may be used if the system is not available.

2-26. Installation physical security inspectors conduct the inspection. They are normally selected by the provost marshal, PSO , or commander and should have the following qualifications:

- Be qualified in the 31B or 31E (if assigned to the United States Disciplinary Barracks) military occupational specialty.
- Be a staff sergeant or above (can be waived to sergeant) or be a civilian employee who meets the current General Schedule-0080 physical security qualification standard for the particular grade assigned to the position (see AR 190-13).
- Complete the Conventional Physical Security Course conducted by USAMPS.
- Be cleared for access to SECRET national defense information.
- Be cleared for a favorable crime records check.
- Possess DA Form 4261/4261-1 (Physical Security Inspector Identification Card).

2-27. Physical security inspectors should not engage in illegal or dangerous conduct that demonstrates security weaknesses. Inspections may be unannounced; however, inspectors should review unit schedules to ensure that inspections do not interfere with training, mobilization, demobilization, or similar requirements.

2-28. All Army assets listed in the AR 190 series should be inspected for compliance with minimum physical protective and security procedural measures. *Security procedural measures* **are physical security measures to counter risk factors that will periodically change over a period of time—such as criminal, terrorist, and hostile threats. The procedures can usually be changed in a short time and involve manpower**.

2-29. Only one inspection report should be recorded, regardless of the number of assets assessed in a single organization. Physical security inspections should be conducted—

- Every 18 months for conventional AA&E (not bulk storage) (see AR 190-11).
- Every 24 months for conventional AA&E bulk storage assets, nuclear reactors, special nuclear materials, chemical agents, and select biological agents and toxins (see AR 190-11 and AR 190-59).
- Every 24 months for other assets (see AR 190-51).
- When a MEVA is identified (see AR 190-13).
- When a unit or activity is activated.

- When no record exists of a prior inspection.
- When there is a change in the unit or activity that may impact existing physical security plans and an indication or a reported incident of significant or recurring criminal activity.
- When the commander determines that greater frequency is required.

Note. Reserve Officer Training Corps regional physical security personnel inspect their facilities during the annual formal inspection (see AR 190-13).

2-30. Physical security inspectors should be granted access to Army facilities, records, and information on a need-to-know basis, consistent with the inspector's clearance for access to defense information and provisions of applicable regulations.

2-31. A copy of the inspection report (with exhibits) should be provided to the commander of the unit or director of the organization, commander or director at the next higher headquarters, and the installation PSO .

2-32. Security deficiencies requiring correction beyond the local commander's capabilities should be reported to the next-higher commander to program resource requirements. The submission of a work order does not resolve a deficiency. Compensatory measures should be employed with available resources until the work order is completed. Recurring deficiencies should be tracked during future physical security inspections until they are corrected. A follow-up inspection should be conducted in 6 months if the initial inspection resulted in an unsatisfactory rating.

2-33. A report of action taken is required for physical security inspections. The report should be provided by the unit commander to the supporting garrison commander. A copy should be maintained by the inspected organization and by the PSO until the next inspection is conducted. Reports are properly classified and safeguarded per AR 380-5.

PHYSICAL SECURITY SYSTEMS

2-34. A physical security system is built on the foundation that baseline security and protection posture are established—based on the local threat, site-specific vulnerabilities, number and type of critical assets, and employment of available resources. To successfully counter threats, physical security systems must be scalable and proportional to increases in the local threat and designed to employ layered defense in depth.

2-35. Physical security measures are a combination of active and passive systems, devices, and security forces that are used to protect an asset or facility from possible threat. These systems and measures include—

- Barrier systems (chapter 4).
- Security lighting (chapter 5).
- Integrated electronic security systems (chapter 6).
- Access control systems (chapters 6 and 7).
- Key and locking systems (chapter 8).
- Security and guard forces (chapter 9).

2-36. The goal of physical security systems is to employ security in depth to preclude or reduce the potential for sabotage, theft, trespass, terrorism, espionage, or other criminal activity. To achieve this goal, each security system component has a function and related measures that provide an integrated capability for—

- **Deterrence.** A potential aggressor who perceives a risk of being caught may be deterred from attacking an asset. The effectiveness of deterrence varies with the aggressor's sophistication, the asset's attractiveness, and the aggressor's objective. Although deterrence is not considered a direct design objective, it may be a result of the design.
- **Detection.** A detection measure senses an act of aggression, assesses the validity of the detection, and communicates the appropriate information to a response force. A detection system must provide all three of these capabilities to be effective. Detection measures may detect an

aggressor's movement via IDSs, or they may detect weapons and tools via X-ray machines or metal or explosive detectors. Detection measures may also include access control elements that assess the validity of identification credentials. These control elements may provide a programmed response (admission or denial), or they may relay information to a response force. Guards serve as detection elements, detecting intrusions and controlling access.

- **Assessment.** Assessment—through the use of video subsystems, patrols, or fixed posts—assists in localizing and determining the size and intent of an unauthorized intrusion or activity.
- **Delay.** Delay measures protect an asset from aggression by delaying or preventing an aggressor's movement toward the asset or by shielding the asset from weapons and explosives. They—
  - Delay aggressors from gaining access by forced entry using tools. These measures include barriers, along with a response force.
  - Prevent an aggressor's movement toward an asset. These measures provide barriers to movement and obscure the line of sight to assets.
  - Protect the asset from the effects of tools, weapons, and explosives.

  Delay measures may be active or passive. Active delay measures are manually or automatically activated in response to acts of aggression. Passive delay measures do not depend on detection or a response—for example, blast-resistant building components and fences. Guards may also be considered delay measures.
- **Response.** Most protective measures depend on response personnel to assess unauthorized acts, report detailed information, and defeat an aggressor. Although defeat is not a design objective, defensive and detection systems must be designed to accommodate (or at least not interfere with) response force activities.

TACTICAL-ENVIRONMENT CONSIDERATIONS

2-37. Fixed sites in tactical environments are especially vulnerable to hazards and threats. Actions against enemy threats and toward other potential emergencies, including natural disasters and accidents, must be planned and adjustments made to protection and security plans. Expeditionary forces may not have initial access to sophisticated electronic security devices and may have to develop field-expedient means of intrusion detection, early warning, and other protection measures. For these forces, enhancement of local security and protection efforts occurs with trip flares, binoculars, night-vision devices, barriers, fences, exterior security lighting, and clear fields of fire.

2-38. As conditions improve and resources become available, other security measures (such as remotely monitored electronic sensors, forward-looking IR systems, and unmanned-aircraft systems) may be used to improve protection. Establishing access control measures, installing concrete barriers and guard towers, and conducting aggressive security patrols can deny enemy access to the area immediately surrounding friendly forces. Whether establishing a new base or occupying an existing one, military leaders should initially focus on establishing or reassessing protective measures at the perimeter of the base. Once these measures are adequate, leaders can then direct attention to the measures used to protect personnel or assets located at the interior of the base.

Note. For additional information on site selection, protection, and security for forward-operating bases, see Graphic Training Aid (GTA) 90-01-011.

2-39. Regardless of the environment or available resources, the protection of Army personnel and assets follow the same general procedures: Identify the asset or area to be protected, determine its mission criticality, assess the likelihood of compromise, assess potential threats and tactics, and develop and implement control measures.

PROTECTION MEASURES FOR CONTRACTORS

2-40. Protecting contractors and their employees in high-threat environments is the commander's responsibility. When contractors perform in potentially hostile or hazardous areas, the supported military forces must ensure the protection of their operations and personnel. The responsibility for ensuring that contractors receive adequate protection starts with the combatant commander and includes subordinate commanders and the contractor (see FM 3-100.21).

2-41. Protection measures for contractor support must be based on the mission, threat, and location. Commanders and planners should determine the need for contractor protection early in the planning process. Commanders assess the local threat and vulnerabilities and assess the risk of using local-national and contractor personnel. The results of the threat and vulnerability assessments are used to develop security plans designed to protect contractors.

2-42. Protection for contractors may involve the use of armed security forces to provide escort or perimeter security and passive measures that include protective barriers, ESSs, and personal self-protection (such as chemical and ballistics protection). Specific security efforts to protect contractors may include—

- Requiring contractors to reside on military bases and facilities.
- Providing escorts, training, protective clothing and equipment.
- Installing physical security systems in and around work sites and living quarters.

2-43. The local PSO should issue identification cards to contractor personnel for entry into all military-controlled areas or facilities. Identification cards aid in the accountability of contractor personnel and help security forces maintain visibility over the contractors in the area—which is necessary to orchestrate their activities and movements so that combat forces are aware of their location.

2-44. The contractor implements and complies with all government-directed management requirements addressed in the contract. The contractor is responsible for ensuring that contract employees comply with DOD, Army, and theater-specific policies and directives.

This page intentionally left blank.

Chapter 3

Site Design Approach

With the development of the security engineering UFC series, the first DOD-wide standardized process for identifying and justifying design criteria beyond the minimum standard was established. The security engineering UFCs provide the regulatory guidance for incorporating security and antiterrorism principles into design criteria for DOD-facility design. The security engineering series includes—

- UFC 4-010-01 and UFC 4-010-02, which establish standards that provide minimum protection measures against terrorist attacks for all DOD-inhabited buildings.
- UFC 4-020-01, which supports the planning of projects, including the requirements for security and antiterrorism.

In addition to the standards, planning, and design UFCs, there is a series of security engineering support manuals that provide specialized, discipline-specific design guidance. (Appendix B provides the appropriate Web site where these and other security-related resources can be accessed.) Intended users of the security engineering series include engineering planners, who are responsible for project development, and protection planning teams, who are responsible for developing design criteria for projects. These projects include new construction, existing construction, and expeditionary and temporary construction. Protection planning teams are based on local considerations, but typically include facility users and antiterrorism, intelligence, operations, security, logistics, engineering, and resource management personnel. This chapter focuses on the physical security issues that may influence the site design of new construction at permanent or expeditionary bases.

INITIAL DESIGN PLANNING CONSIDERATIONS

3-1. The development of a new base or hardening of existing fortifications requires the skills and abilities of engineer personnel. The PSO coordinates with engineers to integrate physical security requirements into site design plans. It is critical to include physical security concerns in the initial master plan to achieve the desired end state for protection at the best possible cost.

3-2. The threat tactic, severity of the attack, and desired level of protection are primary considerations in the initial master design plan. UFC 4-020-01 presents a systematic protective design planning process that evaluates risk based on the likelihood of attack, consequences of the attack, and effectiveness of applied countermeasures in mitigating any attack.

3-3. The PSO participates in the planning process as a member of the protection planning team, with a focus on providing guidance for perimeter security, internal security, and access control. The protection planning team conducts a threat assessment to determine likely aggressors, tactics, tools, weapons, and explosives that may be used against friendly forces. To successfully design protective measures to defeat threats, planners need to know aggressor objectives, categories, and tactics (see UFC 4-020-01).

3-4. There are four major aggressor objectives to consider:

- Inflicting injury or death on people.
- Destroying or damaging facilities, property, equipment, or resources.
- Stealing equipment, material, or information.
- Creating adverse publicity.

3-5. There are four broad categories of aggressors—criminals, protesters, terrorists, and subversives. The hostile acts performed by these aggressors range from crimes to low-intensity conflicts.

3-6. Aggressor tactics include a wide range of offensive strategies that reflect their capabilities and objectives. UFC 4-020-01 categorizes these offensive strategies into 12 tactics that are specific methods of achieving aggressor goals. Separating these tactics into categories allows facility planners to define threats in common terms that can be used by facility designers and security personnel. Aggressor tactics include —

- Vehicle bomb (moving or stationary).
- Hand-delivered device attack.
- Indirect-fire weapon.
- Direct-fire weapon.
- Airborne contamination.
- Waterborne contamination.
- Waterfront attack.
- Forced entry.
- Covert entry.
- Visual surveillance.
- Acoustic eavesdropping.
- Electronic-emanation eavesdropping.

PERIMETER SECURITY

3-7. The perimeter security system is often the first line of defense, and it provides a visual deterrent to potential adversaries. Perimeter security should be designed to incorporate the concept of layered defense in depth and integrate security elements such as barriers, lighting, intrusion detection, surveillance systems, and access control equipment.

3-8. The design of the perimeter security systems should meet the following requirements:

- Provide adequate blast-standoff distances (see UFC 4-010-01 and 4-010-02).
- Limit or block the line of sight from outside vantage points.
- Provide sufficient room for vehicle and pedestrian access control.
- Maximize the threat ingress/egress time across the exterior site.
- Enhance the ability of security forces to observe threats before they can attack.

3-9. Depending on the asset to be protected and the resources available, commanders should develop security protective measures from the asset to the perimeter or from the perimeter to the asset.

STANDOFF DISTANCE

3-10. The best technique to reduce the risks and effects of an enemy attack is to provide adequate distance between the inhabited structure and the attack. The standoff distance is the maintained distance between where a potential attack occurs and the intended target. The PSO should be familiar with the minimum standoff distances established in UFC 4-010-01 and UFC 4-010-02. These distances should be a primary consideration for recommending the location of critical assets, inhabited structures, and restricted facilities. Table 3-1 provides standoff distances for new and existing buildings.

Table 3-1. Standoff distances for new and existing buildings

Location	Building Category	Standoff Distance or Separation Requirements			
		Applicable Level of Protection	Conventional Construction Standoff Distance	Minimum Standoff Distance[1]	Applicable Explosive Weight[2]
Controlled perimeter or parking and roadways without a controlled perimeter	Billeting and high-occupancy family housing	Low	45 m[3] (148 ft)	25 m[3] (82 ft)	I
	Primary gathering building	Low	45 m[3,4] (148 ft)	25 m[3,4] (82 ft)	I
	Inhabited building	Very low	25 m[3] (82 ft)	10 m[3] (33 ft)	I
Parking and roadways within a controlled perimeter	Billeting and high-occupancy family housing	Low	25 m[3] (82 ft)	10 m[3] (33 ft)	II
	Primary gathering building	Low	25 m[3,4] (82 ft)	10 m[3,4] (33 ft)	II
	Inhabited building	Very low	10 m[3] (33 ft)	10 m[3] (33 ft)	II
Trash containers	Billeting and high-occupancy family housing	Low	25 m (82 ft)	10 m (33 ft)	II
	Primary gathering building	Low	25 m (82 ft)	10 m (33 ft)	II
	Inhabited building	Very low	10 m (33 ft)	10 m (33 ft)	II

[1]Even with analysis, standoff distances less than those in this column are not allowed for new buildings, but are allowed for existing buildings if constructed/retrofitted to provide the required level of protection at the reduced standoff distance.
[2]See UFC 4-010-02 for specific explosive weights (kilograms/pounds of trinitrotoluene) associated with designations I and II.
[3]For existing buildings, see paragraph B-1.1.2.2 in UFC 4-010-01 for additional options.
[4]For existing family housing, see paragraph B-1.1.2.2.3 in UFC 4-010-01 for additional options.

Legend:
ft	feet
m	meter
UFC	unified facilities criteria

Source: UFC 4-010-01.

3-11. Standoff distances must be coupled with appropriate building hardening to provide the necessary level of protection. Where necessary, standoff distance may be increased to reduce the blast effects on a structure. The required standoff distances will vary with building components used in the construction.

3-12. Blast pressures near an exploding vehicle bomb are very high, but they decrease rapidly with increased standoff distance. Maximizing the standoff distance is the primary design strategy. Maximizing standoff distance also ensures that there is opportunity in the future to upgrade buildings to meet increased threats or to accommodate higher levels of protection. Where standoff distances cannot be achieved because land is unavailable, the standards allow for building hardening to mitigate the blast effects.

PHYSICAL BARRIERS

3-13. Physical barriers are an integral part of the perimeter security system and serve to facilitate the control of pedestrian and vehicle access. Physical barriers define the perimeter and establish a physical and psychological deterrent to adversaries attempting unlawful or unauthorized entry. Physical barriers delay and disrupt an attack and channel the flow of personnel and vehicles through designated ACPs. Two types of physical barriers should be considered—natural and manmade.

3-14. It may be impossible to build a protective barrier that cannot be penetrated by a human or heavy armor. Therefore, as opposed to protecting a facility using only one barrier, enhance security by using a combination of barriers to increase delay. Multiple barriers cause aggressors to expend more energy trying to breach all of the barriers, and they provide the appearance of additional security that may further deter some aggressors.

3-15. Initially, expeditionary forces may have to take advantage of natural barriers such as mountains, swamps, thick vegetation, rivers, bays, and cliffs. As conditions improve, more permanent physical barriers are constructed to provide better protection. Manmade barriers include fences, walls, gates, and various types of vehicle barriers (see chapter 4).

SECURITY LIGHTING

3-16. Security forces need to see for long distances at different low-level light contrasts, identify indistinct outlines of silhouettes, and be able to spot an intruder whose silhouette may only be exposed to view for a matter of seconds. Adequate lighting improves the ability of security forces to detect intruders before they attack.

3-17. Security lighting should be designed to—
- Enhance threat detection, assessment, and interdiction.
- Serve as a deterrent.
- Increase the effectiveness of the security force and ESSs by increasing the visibility range.

3-18. Lighting should not be used alone; it should supplement other measures of protection, such as security forces, patrols, fences, and electronic surveillance systems. Security lighting is most effective when it adequately provides glaring light in the eyes of the intruder but does not illuminate security forces. The types of perimeter lighting include—
- Continuous lighting.
- Glare lighting.
- Standby lighting.
- Emergency lighting.
- Motion-activated lighting.

3-19. ACPs should be provided with multiple, redundant lighting sources to ensure that the loss of a single system does not seriously interrupt operations or place security forces at risk.

Note. Chapter 5 provides detailed guidance for security lighting techniques and requirements.

INTRUSION DETECTION AND SURVEILLANCE SYSTEMS

3-20. The function of perimeter IDS is to detect a threat and initiate a response by security personnel. Although not a requirement, IDS can enhance perimeter security. IDS and electronic surveillance systems facilitate more economical and efficient use of security personnel and provide additional controls at critical areas or points. IDS enhances the capability of the security force to detect and defeat intruders and provides the early warning of unlawful or unauthorized access to protected areas.

Note. UFC 4-021-02NF provides ways to establish and implement design criteria for ESSs.

3-21. The IDS and surveillance system should provide functional capabilities that include threat detection, annunciation, assessment, and classification. Other integrated security systems and personnel perform threat delay and threat response. The PSO identifies IDS requirements early in the design planning process once the site has been selected and the base layout plan has been developed. The performance parameters of the system should include—

- Completeness of coverage.
- False and nuisance alarm rates.
- Probability of detection.
- Zone at which the alarm occurred.
- Delay time.

3-22. Currently, there are several types of IDS sensors in use throughout the Army (see chapter 6). Common types of IDS sensors include—

- Passive IR.
- Active IR.
- Microwave radar.
- Near-IR beam break.
- Fence-mounted.
- Taut wire.
- Ground motion.
- Ported coaxial cable.
- Seismic.
- Acoustic.
- Magnetic.
- Break wire.
- Electrostatic field.

3-23. Regardless of the operational environment, commanders should initially focus on developing protective measures at the perimeter to establish a secure inner area.

SECURITY TOWERS

3-24. The design of guard towers and overwatch positions must begin with a physical site study, including terrain analysis, and an analysis of security requirements. Based on this data, basic design considerations include—

- Accommodations for the maximum number of personnel required in the tower.
- Required number of towers.
- Location and height of the tower that best supports the base.
- Requirement for electronic and communications equipment.
- Location of gun ports.
- Climate-control and plumbing requirements.
- Small arms protection based on the threat assessment.

- Methods for security personnel to transmit under duress to other security forces.
- Manually operated searchlights.
- Ability to hear activity in the area of the tower.

3-25. The height of a tower increases the range of observation during daylight hours and at night with artificial illumination. However, during inclement weather and during a blackout, towers lose this advantage and must be supplemented by on-ground observation.

INSTALLATION ACCESS CONTROL POINTS

3-26. The number of installation ACPs in active use should be limited to the minimum number required for safe and efficient operations. When necessary, install vehicle barriers in front of vehicle gates. Security lighting is required at all access points.

Note. Refer to UFC 4-020-01 for the application and selection of vehicle barriers.

3-27. Active perimeter entrances should be designated so that security forces maintain full control without an unnecessary delay in traffic. This is accomplished by having sufficient entrances to accommodate the peak flow of pedestrian and vehicular traffic and by having adequate lighting for rapid and efficient inspections. When ACPs are not operational, they should be securely locked, illuminated during hours of darkness, and periodically inspected by a roving patrol. Additionally, warning signs should be used to alert drivers when gates are closed. Doors and windows on buildings that form a part of the perimeter should be locked, lighted, and inspected.

3-28. ACPs are provided at main perimeter entrances where security personnel are present. Considerations for their construction and use should be based on the information outlined in UFC 4-022-01 and the Army Standard Definitive Design for ACPs.

3-29. ACPs should be located as close as practical to the perimeter entrance so that personnel inside the station can maintain constant surveillance over the entrance and its approaches. Additional considerations at entry control stations include—

- Establishing a holding area for unauthorized vehicles or those to be further inspected. A turnaround area should be provided to avoid impeding other traffic.
- Establishing control measures, such as displaying a decal on the window or having a specially marked vehicle.

3-30. ACPs that are manned 24 hours per day should have interior and exterior lighting, interior heating (where appropriate), and a sufficient glassed area to afford adequate observation for personnel inside. Where appropriate, entry control stations should be designed for optimum personnel identification and movement control. Each station should also include a telephone, a radio, and badge racks (if required).

Note. Chapter 7 provides detailed information on access control procedures.

WARNING SIGNS

3-31. Signs should be erected to assist in controlling authorized entry, deter unauthorized entry, and preclude accidental entry. Signs should be plainly displayed and be legible from any approach to the perimeter from a reasonable distance. The size and coloring of a sign, its letters, and the interval of posting must be appropriate to each situation.

3-32. Warning signs augment control signs. They warn intruders that the area is restricted and that trespassing may result in the use of deadly force. The signs should be posted at intervals of no more than 100 feet.

3-33. Warning signs should be installed along the physical barriers of the controlled area and at each entry point where they can be seen readily and understood by anyone approaching the perimeter. In areas where English is one of two or more languages commonly spoken, warning signs must contain the local language in addition to English. The wording on the signs will denote warning of a restricted area. Additionally, the warning signs prescribed in AR 190-13 should be posted at all entrances to restricted areas within the boundaries of the base.

PERIMETER ROADS AND CLEAR ZONES

3-34. When the perimeter barrier encloses a large area, an interior, all-weather perimeter road should be provided for security patrol vehicles. Clear zones should be maintained on both sides of the perimeter barrier to provide an unobstructed view of the barrier and the ground adjacent to it. Roads in the clear zone should be as close to the perimeter barrier as possible without interfering with it. The roads should be constructed to allow effective road barriers to deter motor movement of unauthorized personnel during mobilization periods.

3-35. Clear zones should be kept clear of weeds, rubbish, or other material that offers concealment or assistance to an intruder attempting to breach the barrier. A clear zone of 20 feet or more should exist between the perimeter barrier and exterior structures, parking areas, and natural or manmade features. When possible, a clear zone of 50 feet or more should exist between the perimeter barrier and structures within the protected area, except when a wall of a building constitutes part of the perimeter barrier. An ammunition supply point should have clear zones 12 feet outside the ammunition supply point and 30 feet inside; the vegetation will not exceed 8 inches (4 inches for high-threat and highly controlled areas).

Note. See AR 190-11 and DOD O-2000.12-H for further information.

3-36. When it is impossible to have adequate clear zones because of property lines or natural or manmade features, it may be necessary to increase the height of the perimeter barrier, increase security patrol coverage, add more security lighting, or install an intrusion detection device along that portion of the perimeter.

INTERNAL SECURITY

3-37. Internal security consists of those measures designed to protect personnel and assets located on the interior of the base. The PSO assists the staff in the protection cell in integrating internal security procedures. This ensures that security measures and systems are synchronized with a coherent protection strategy.

3-38. The PSO assesses internal security requirements that include security forces, roving patrols, interior guards, and MWD support. In conjunction with the physical security measures employed on the perimeter, a well-trained and -equipped security force is one of the most effective resources in a comprehensive protection plan.

3-39. Determining the type, size, and composition of the security force requires an assessment of the—
- Threat.
- Size, location, and geographical characteristics of the base.
- Mission.
- Type, number, and size of restricted areas.
- Use and effectiveness of physical security equipment, measures, and barriers.
- Available manpower.
- Base population and composition.
- Criticality of assets being protected.

3-40. The PSO determines the specific security post requirements and operating procedures and develops special written instructions and security force checklists. Security force orders should be specifically written for each post and should describe the guard's duties in detail. The order should be brief, clear, concise, and specific. Security orders should contain the following information:

- Special orders for each post, including specific limits of the post; duties to be performed; hours of operation; and required uniform, arms, and equipment.
- Specific instructions in the application and use of deadly force and detailed guidance in the safe handling of weapons.
- Training requirements for security personnel and designated posts.
- Security force chain of command.

3-41. Checklists should be developed and maintained at each guard post. Checklists should include standing rules for the use of force, procedures for the escalation of force, scenarios for the rules of engagement (ROE), daily intelligence briefs, and range cards. Checklists should help guards identify threats, decide when to take action, and determine the appropriate action. For example, the checklist should explain the procedures for initiating a base-wide alert.

Chapter 4

Protective Barriers

Protective barriers are an integral part of all physical security systems and are used to define the physical limits of an installation, activity, or area. Barriers restrict, channel, impede access, or shield activities within the installation from immediate, direct observation, and they are fully integrated with other protective measures to form continuous obstacles around the installation. Barriers should be focused on providing assets with an acceptable level of protection/deterrence against the worst-case threat. Barriers become platforms on which more sophisticated sensors can be placed to aid in threat detection and classification. UFC 4-022-02 provides the design requirements necessary to plan, design, construct, and maintain protective barriers used as perimeter protection. Interior use of barriers is essential for protection of critical infrastructures, such as water treatment and storage facilities and power and heating plants. Restricted areas such as command and control centers, ammunition storage sites, and communication centers require barriers for security and safety standards.

BARRIER EMPLACEMENT CONSIDERATIONS

4-1.   Protective barriers form the perimeter of controlled areas and serve to facilitate control of pedestrian and vehicle ingress and egress. Barriers should be emplaced in concert with each other, the natural terrain, and any manmade obstructions. Combinations or layers of barriers are most effective and provide defense in depth. Barriers should afford an equal degree of continuous protection along the entire perimeter.

4-2.   The placement of barriers should maximize standoff distances. Perimeter barriers should be located as far as possible from critical assets and inhabited buildings to mitigate blast effects. Barriers should be positioned away from other structures such as trees, telephone poles, or adjacent buildings that may be used as aids to circumvent the barrier. They should not be placed where vehicles can park immediately adjacent to them. This situation creates a platform from which aggressors can mount an attack. Additional toppings on barriers such as concertina, razor, or barbed wire inhibit aggressor efforts to vault or scale the top of the barrier.

4-3.   Barriers offer important benefits to the overall physical security posture and have a direct impact on the number of security posts needed; however, barriers cannot be designed for all situations. Considerations for protective structural barriers include weighing the cost of completely enclosing large tracts of land with significant structural barriers against the threat and the cost of alternate security precautions (such as patrols, MWD, ground sensors, electronic surveillance, and airborne sensors).

4-4.   A layered approach should be used when planning for the emplacement of barriers. Combinations or layers of barriers should be separated by a minimum of 10 meters for optimum protection and control. An unobstructed area or clear zone should be maintained on both sides of, and between, physical barriers. Figure 4-1 page 4-2, illustrates the layered security concept.

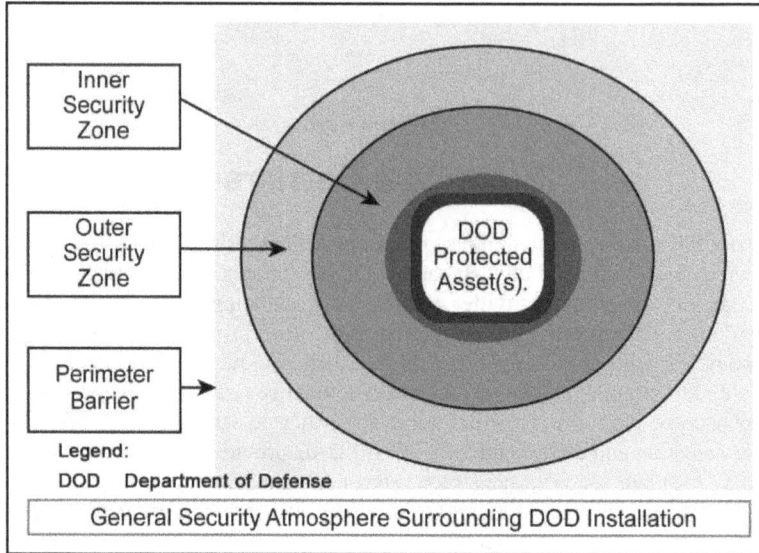

Figure 4-1. Layered security approach

4-5. If a secured area requires a controlled, limited, or exclusion area on a temporary or infrequent basis, it may not be possible to use physical structural barriers. A controlled area is that portion of a restricted area usually near or surrounding an exclusion or limited area. Entry to the controlled area is restricted to authorized personnel. However, movement of authorized personnel in this area is not necessarily controlled. Mere entry to the area does not provide access to the security interest or other matter with the exclusion or limited area. A limited area is a restricted area containing a security interest or other matter in which uncontrolled movement will permit access to such security interest or matter. An exclusion area is a restricted area containing a security interest or other matter of such nature that access to the area constitutes access to such security interest (see AR 190-13).

4-6. A temporary limited or exclusion area may be established where the lack of proper physical barriers is compensated for by additional security posts, patrols, and other security measures during the period of restriction. Temporary barriers (including temporary fences, coiled concertina wire, and vehicles) may be used. Barriers are not the only restrictive element, and they may not always be necessary. They may not be ideal when working with limited or exclusion areas or when integrated with other controls.

4-7. When determining barrier construction or placement, remember that barriers can be compromised. This compromise can be manmade through breaching (cutting a hole through a wall or fence) or by nature (berms eroded by the wind and rain). Consider the following natural effects on barriers during the planning phase:

- Snow or sand can drift against a barrier, making the barrier easy to cross, or it can be deep enough that an intruder may tunnel near the barrier and move undetected by the security force.
- Vegetation such as bushes and trees can provide cover and concealment for intruders. They can also provide means to breach or scale the barrier.
- Rain can soften the ground around barriers, allowing tunnels or trenches to be dug under the barriers.
- Inclement weather such as fog, heavy rain, or snow that limits the visibility of the barrier will provide intruders the opportunity to breach the barrier unseen by the security force.

4-8. Barriers should be inspected and maintained on a routine basis. Security force personnel should look for deliberate breaches, holes in and under barriers, sand dunes or snow drifts building up against barriers, and the proper functioning of locks. Inspection and maintenance costs should be considered during the planning phase to ensure that these functions are included in the overall resource requirements.

4-9. Table 4-1 provides various protective barrier functions and examples to consider.

Table 4-1. Protective barrier functions and examples

Barrier Function	Natural Obstacle	Manmade Obstacle
Establish boundary	River, valley, forest line	Walls, fences, hedges
Isolate activity or discourage visitors	Mountains or hills, jungle, dense growth, desert	Walls, fences, berms, canals, moats
Aid detection of unauthorized entry or intrusion	Not applicable	Electronic detection and surveillance devices mounted on boundary
Impede pedestrian passage	Rivers, swamps, natural terrain features	Fences and walls with or without doors or gates
Impede vehicle passage	Rivers, swamps, natural terrain features	Fences, walls, concrete barriers, 3/4-inch stranded carbon steel wire rope, and bollards
Prevent external visual observation	Forests, natural terrain features	Berms, earthworks, walls, solid fences, masonry-block screens, translucent glass blocks, shutters, awnings, draperies
Minimize ballistic-material penetration	Not applicable	High berms, earthworks, steel-reinforced concrete or solid-fill masonry walls, blast shields fabricated from steel-ply materials, ballistic-resistant glazing

VEHICLE BARRIERS

4-10. The PSO should be familiar with the provisions of UFC 4-022-01, UFC 4-022-02, and the Army ACPs standard design/criteria. These documents provide the regulatory guidance for planning access control activities and employing protective barriers. The national standard for crash testing of perimeter barriers is established in the American Society for Testing and Materials (ASTM) F 2656-07.

4-11. The PSO focuses on the requirements of the security force and the placement of supporting security systems that are integrated into the overall vehicle barrier plan. Understanding the overarching concept of employing vehicle barriers ensures that the needs of the security force are met and that security systems are employed in the most cost-effective manner.

4-12. Vehicle barriers are designed to impede or stop vehicles attempting to pass through perimeters. They can be employed against stationary or moving-vehicle bomb threats. Stationary bomb threats normally require the aggressor to park the vehicle in an authorized parking space and remain unnoticed. Moving-vehicle bomb threats require the vehicle to penetrate through the barrier by ramming at a high rate of speed.

4-13. Vehicle barriers can be breached, but successful breaching methods require considerable time and equipment. Vehicle barrier design and selection factors should include the following:

- Explosive threat.
- Weight of the threat vehicle.
- Sufficient standoff distance between the planned barrier and critical structures.
- Expected speed of the threat vehicle.
- Ability to reduce threat vehicle speed.
- Number of access points requiring vehicle barriers.
- Most cost-effective barrier available that will absorb the kinetic energy developed by the threat vehicle.
- Availability of security forces for constant surveillance/observation.
- Temporary or permanent nature of the barrier.

PASSIVE VEHICLE BARRIERS

4-14. Passive barriers are typically heavy constructed barriers and are not easily moved or relocated. They require no action once in place and are normally used to direct and channel the flow of traffic at the ACP. Passive barriers are ideal for defining the boundary of the perimeter and establishing a minimum standoff distance against a stationary bomb threat. Used at the outer perimeter, a passive vehicle barrier can be hardened to resist a moving-vehicle bomb threat.

4-15. For the moving-vehicle bomb tactic, the barriers are heavy structures and have many construction and operations considerations associated with them. These barriers are commercially available to stop various vehicles at different speeds up to a 15,000-pound truck traveling 50 miles per hour (see UFC 4-022-02).

4-16. Placement of passive vehicle barriers should be focused along high-speed avenues of approach outside the perimeter. When selecting the type of barrier, give consideration to secondary debris and fragmentation created by explosives in close proximity to concrete barriers or concrete walls. Typical passive vehicle barriers include the concrete Jersey barrier, used for countermobility.

4-17. The Jersey barrier can be employed for countermobility around ACPs; however, the barrier is not effective in stopping primary debris and may become secondary debris in the immediate vicinity of a large explosion. Instead of protecting personnel and assets from blast or fragment damage, concrete barriers can cause additional damage by becoming secondary debris.

4-18. Jersey barriers should not be used to mitigate blast damage and should be connected with cables if they are intended to stop moving vehicles. If they are used as perimeter barriers for the stationary-vehicle bomb tactic or to channel or impede vehicle movement, they do not need to be connected. Figure 4-2 shows a typical Jersey barrier. Figure 4-3 shows a cable and anchoring system used with the lightweight concrete Jersey barrier.

Figure 4-2. Jersey barrier

Figure 4-3. Jersey barriers connected with a cabling and anchor system

ACTIVE VEHICLE BARRIERS

4-19. Active barriers are normally located at facility entrances, entry gates to restricted areas, or selected interior locations. Placement of active vehicle barriers may vary; however, in each case the barrier should be located as far from the critical structure as practical to minimize damage due to possible blast effects. Likewise, support equipment such as generators, batteries, and hydraulic power systems should be located on the secure side and away from guard posts to lower the threat of sabotage and injury to security personnel. These barriers require some action by personnel, equipment, or both to prevent entry of a vehicle. Active barriers should be combined with obstacles on the approach roadway, such as serpentines and speed bumps to force vehicles to slow down to a speed that can be stopped by barriers.

4-20. An active vehicle barrier is capable of inflicting serious injury when activated inadvertently. Warning signs, lights, bells, and bright colors should be used to mark the presence of a barrier and make it visible to oncoming traffic. Pedestrian traffic should be channeled away from the barrier. For high-volume traffic flow, vehicle barriers are normally open, allowing vehicles to pass, and activated when a threat has been detected. Security forces should be able to activate and close the barrier before the threat vehicle can reach it. Where threat conditions are high, barriers are normally closed and opened only after authorization has been verified. For additional information regarding the location and operation of vehicle barriers, see UFC 4-022-01.

4-21. Typical active barriers include retractable bollards, sliding gates, and wooden gates that can be raised and lowered. Actual vehicle barrier standards and performance levels are established in the Unified Facilities Guide Specifications (UFGS) 34 71 13.19. Figure 4-4, page 4-6, illustrates several active vehicle barriers.

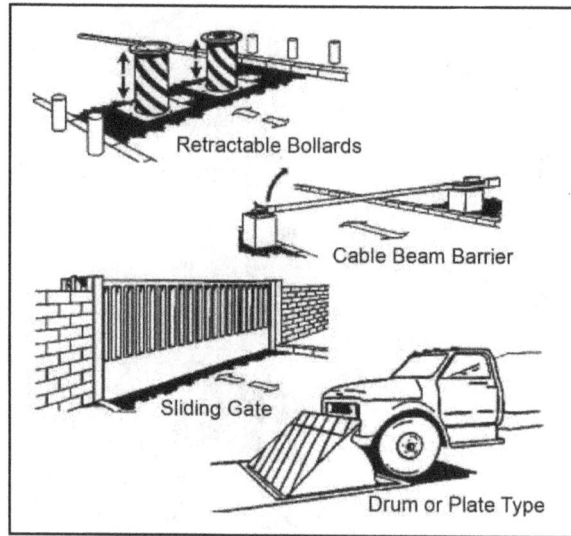

Figure 4-4. Active vehicle barriers

EARTH-FILLED BARRIERS

4-22. Earth-filled barriers are typically employed around expeditionary structures to provide blast and fragment damage protection, and consist of things like earth berms, container walls, and sandbags. As fragment protection, these barrier types work extremely well; however, for blast mitigation purposes, these barriers will reduce structural damage only slightly by reducing reflected pressures to incident pressure levels. Reflected pressure is the pressure of the blast wave that occurs when it impacts a wall or vertical surface perpendicular to it. Incident pressure is the pressure of the blast wave out in the open before it hits a reflective surface and on vertical and horizontal surfaces that are not perpendicular to the blast wave, such as side and rear walls and roofs.

4-23. When used as vehicle barriers, earth-filled barriers—such as soil bins—are normally built with a two-row-wide base and at least a second level to provide sufficient mass to stop a moving vehicle bomb threat.

4-24. Figure 4-5 illustrates sandbags employed for blast protection. Sandbags, which are intended for fragmentation mitigation, can be used behind container barriers to reduce secondary debris hazard associated with spalling concrete. When implemented correctly, they may be used to mitigate blast damage and have the advantage of not creating significant secondary debris if located near an exploding vehicle bomb.

Figure 4-5. Sandbags employed for blast protection

4-25. Figure 4-6 illustrates container-style barriers used for blast and fragment mitigation. These barriers work well as fragment protection and can reduce blast effects on a protected structure. Employment techniques are for countermobility, blast walls, or fighting positions.

Figure 4-6. Container-style barriers

4-26. Figure 4-7, page 4-8, illustrates soil-backed barriers used for critical asset protection; they may also be used for limited fragment and blast mitigation.

Figure 4-7. Soil-backed container-style barrier

FENCING

4-27. Three types of fencing are authorized for use in protecting restricted areas—chain link, barbed wire, and barbed tape or concertina. The type used for construction depends primarily on the threat and the degree of permanence. It may also depend on the availability of materials and the time available for construction. Fencing may be erected for other uses besides impeding personnel access; it can impede observation, reduce the effectiveness of standoff-weapon systems, and serve as a barrier to hand-thrown weapons (such as grenades and firebombs).

4-28. Generally, chain-link fencing will be used for protecting permanent limited and exclusion areas. All three types of fencing may be used to augment or increase the security of existing fences that protect restricted areas—for example, to create an additional barrier line, to increase existing fence height, or to provide other methods that effectively add to physical security. It is important to recognize that fencing provides very little delay when it comes to motivated aggressors, but it can act as a psychological deterrent—especially when integrated with other security systems, such as security lights, electronic surveillance, and frequent patrolling.

CHAIN LINK

4-29. Chain-link fences (including gates) must be constructed of a minimum of 6-foot material, excluding the top guard. Fence heights for conventional arms and ammunition security must be a minimum of 6 feet for standard chain-link, wire-mesh fencing. Chain-link fences must be constructed with 9-gauge or heavier wire, be zinc coated, and have a mesh opening not larger than 2 inches per side, with twisted and barbed top selvages and knuckled bottom selvage. The wire must be taut and securely fastened to rigid metal posts set in concrete and must reach within 2 inches of hard ground or pavement. On soft ground, the wire must reach below the surface deep enough to compensate for shifting soil or sand, and proper erosion control measures should be considered. Materials and construction must meet with the standards described in UFGS 32 31 13. 53.

4-30. Fence fabric should be mounted on steel posts. Tension wires will either be interwoven or clipped along the top and bottom row of fabric diamonds. The wire fabric will be secured to posts and tension wires as specified in Federal Specification (FS) RR-F-191/4. When a more secure manner of attaching the fabric to posts is desired, a power-driven fabric and wire fastener may be used. Provide wire ties constructed of the same material as the fencing fabric; provide accessories with polyvinyl coatings similar to that specified for chain-link fabric or framework. If the ties or fasteners are coated or plated, the coating or plating must be electrolytically compatible with the fence fabric to inhibit corrosion.

4-31. Weaknesses in the chain-link fence occur as a result of weather (rusting) or failure to keep it fastened to the post that affects the desired tightness. Damage to the fence and fence fabric may be the result of allowing vegetation and trees to grow on or near the fence. The interaction between the fence and the overgrowth often leads to fence damage and reduces the integrity and continuity of the fence as a perimeter boundary and barrier.

4-32. Another weakness of chain link is that the fabric can prevent observation from cameras or stationary guards at certain angles. The links will provide a visual effect of a solid wall of chain link depending on the angle of observation. Chain link also affects air circulation around generators. Security planners should consider this visual effect when planning static guard posts, towers or camera emplacements.

BARBED-WIRE SPECIFICATIONS

4-33. Standard barbed wire is twisted, double-strand, 12.5-gauge wire, zinc- or aluminum-coated, with four-point barbs spaced no more than 5 inches apart. Barbed-wire fences (including gates) intended to prevent human trespassing should not be less than 6 feet high and must be affixed firmly to posts not more than 6 feet apart. The distance between strands should not exceed 6 inches, and at least one wire should be interlaced vertically and located midway between posts. The ends should be staggered or fastened together, and the base wire should be picketed to the ground. All material and construction should meet UFGS 32 31 13.53.

BARBED TAPE OR CONCERTINA

4-34. A barbed-tape obstacle is fabricated from 0.025-inch stainless steel and is available in 24-, 30-, 40-, and 60-inch-diameter coils. The barbs have a minimum length of 1.2 inches, and the barbed cluster's width is 1.21 inches. All materials should meet UFGS 32 31 13.53. A barbed-tape obstacle deploys tangle-free for fast installation. It may be recovered and reused. Fifty feet (plus or minus 2 inches) can be covered by 101 coil loops. Handling barbed tape requires the use of heavy barbed-tape gauntlets instead of standard barbed-wire gauntlets.

4-35. The most common mistakes security forces make in constructing concertina fences are spacing engineer stakes too far apart, not using intermediate short pickets, neglecting to add horizontal wire, and failing to tie the concertina together (see MIL-HDBK-1013/10).

Barbed-Tape Concertina

4-36. Barbed-tape concertina (standard concertina barbed tape) is a commercially manufactured wire coil of high-strength-steel barbed wire that is clipped together at intervals to form a cylinder. When opened, it is 50 feet long and 3 feet in diameter. When used as the perimeter barrier for a restricted area, the concertina must be laid between poles with one roll on top of another or in a pyramid arrangement (with a minimum of three rolls).

4-37. Reinforced barbed-tape concertina consists of a single strand of spring-steel wire and a single strand of barbed tape. The sections between barbs of the barbed tape are securely clinched around the wire. Each coil is about 37 ½ inches in diameter and consists of 55 spiral turns connected by steel clips to form a cylindrical diamond pattern when extended to a coil length of 50 feet. One end turn is fitted with four bundling wires for securing the coil when closed, and each end turn is fitted with two steel carrying loops. The concertina extends to 50 feet without permanent distortion. When released, it can be retracted into a closed coil.

Top Guard

4-38. When possible, a top guard should be constructed on all perimeter fences and may be added on interior enclosures for additional protection. A top guard (see figures 4-8, 4-9, and 4-10, page 4-10) is an overhang of barbed wire or tape along the top of a fence, facing outward and upward at about a 45-degree angle. Placing barbed wire or tape above it can further enhance the top guard. Top-guard supporting arms will be permanently affixed to the top of fence posts to increase the overall height of the fence by at least 1 foot. (Due to liability issues in some locations, the top guards will not be allowed to face outward where the fence is adjacent to public areas.) Three strands of barbed wire spaced 6 inches apart should be installed on the supporting arms. The number of strands of wire or tape may be increased when required.

4-39. The top guard of fencing adjoining gates may range from a vertical height of 18 inches to the normal 45-degree outward protection, but only for sufficient distance along the fence to open the gates adequately. Bottom and top tension wires should be used in lieu of fence rails. A concrete sill may be cast at the bottom of the fence to protect against soil erosion. A bottom rail is used on high-security fences to prevent intruders from lifting the fence.

Figure 4-8. Single top guard barbed tape

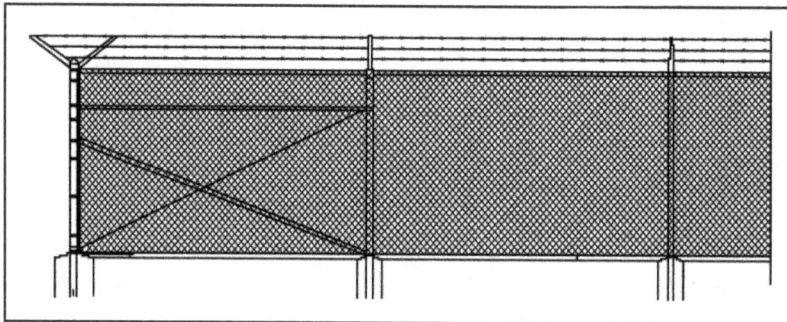

Figure 4-9. Double top guard

Figure 4-10. Double top guard enhanced with concertina or barbed tape

Gates and Entrances

4-40. The number of gates and perimeter entrances must be the minimum required for safe and efficient operation of the facility. Active perimeter entrances must be designed so that the guard force maintains full control. Semiactive entrances, such as infrequently used vehicular gates, must be locked on the inside when not in use. When closed, gates and entrances must provide a barrier structurally comparable to their associated barriers. Care must be afforded against the ability to crawl under gates or jump over portions of the fence where the gate meets with the fence end posts. Top guards, which may be vertical, are required for all gates.

Triple-Standard Concertina Wire

4-41. This type of fence uses three rolls of stacked concertina securely attached to pickets placed on both sides of the two rolls resting on the ground at two paces (approximately 5 feet) from the anchor picket and five paces (approximately 12.5 feet) from the supporting pickets. Taut horizontal-support barbed wire must be attached to pickets above the two rolls resting on the ground to preclude easy removal. One roll will be stacked and securely tied with wire ties on top of two rolls that run parallel to each other while resting on the ground, forming a pyramid. In many situations, this fence has been used effectively in place of a chain-link fence. (If perimeter fencing consists of triple-standard concertina, a top guard is not feasible.) All material and construction should meet the requirements listed in FM 5-34.

Tangle-Foot Wire

4-42. Barbed wire or tape may be used in appropriate situations to construct a tangle-foot obstruction, either outside a single perimeter fence or in the area between double fences, to provide an additional deterrent to intruders. The wire or tape should be supported on short metal or wooden pickets, spaced at irregular intervals of 3 to 10 feet and at heights between 6 and 12 inches. The wire or tape should be crisscrossed to provide a more effective obstacle, and the base wire must be picketed to the ground at irregular intervals. The space and materials available govern the depth of the field.

INTERIOR BARRIERS

4-43. Interior barriers may be in the form of a physical barrier or through the implementation of access control measures or devices. Barriers may be used in the interior of facilities to accomplish the same functions performed by an installation's perimeter barriers. Interior barriers establish boundaries or lines of demarcation of different activities (and differing levels of security) within a facility. They deter and intimidate individuals who attempt unauthorized entry. As in the case of perimeter barriers, interior barriers are platforms on which intrusion detection sensors or surveillance systems can be mounted.

4-44. Barriers may be used in a facility to channel pedestrian and service-vehicle traffic. In addition, use of high-security doors, window glazing, and walls can provide building occupants with protection against ballistic penetrations such as bomb fragments and broken glass.

INTERIOR BARRIER MATERIALS

4-45. An infinite range of materials and construction techniques is available to help security planners meet specific needs. Materials and techniques used to enhance the building exterior's resistance to penetration can also be applied in a building. Table 4-2, page 4-12, illustrates some of the materials that can be used to erect barriers in a facility and the relationships that exist among the materials used, the type of construction technique used, and the specific barrier function to be performed.

4-46. Use of multiple barrier materials and construction techniques can sometimes accomplish one-barrier purpose with less expensive and less disruptive construction techniques. For example, use of ballistic-resistant, glass-clad polycarbonate panels accompanied by overt surveillance cameras, warning signs, and annunciator devices (such as flashing lights and buzzers) can create an intimidating picture of a high-security barrier adjacent to a high-security passageway. The cost is equal to, or less than, the construction of a reinforced masonry wall to accomplish the same purpose. Consideration should be taken when employing methods that tie in with, or incorporate into, an existing security system. When two security systems are not properly matched or integrated, the overall cost to later modify them for compatibility can be enormous.

4-47. Buildings less than two stories high that form part of a perimeter must have a top guard along the outside edge to deny access to the roof. Masonry walls used as part of a perimeter barrier must be at least 7 feet high and have a barbed-wire top guard. The top guard should be sloped outward at a 45-degree angle and carry at least three strands of barbed wire. This will increase the vertical height of the barrier by at least 1 foot.

4-48. Protect windows, active doors, and other designated openings by securely fastening bars, grilles, or chain-link screens. Fasten window barriers from the inside. If hinged, the hinges and locks must be on the inside. If hinges are on the outside, weld or peen the hinge to eliminate tampering or removal of the hinge pin. Building elements that provide delay against forced entry have stringent requirements. These elements should be designed according to UFC 4-020-01.

Table 4-2. Selected facility barrier materials

	Barrier Function					
	Selected Permanent and Temporary Barrier Materials	Establish Boundaries	Deter Unauthorized Entry	Detect with IDS or Surveillance Sensor Platform	Prevent Visual Observation	Channel Pedestrian and Vehicle Traffic
1.	Reinforced masonry wall, full height	P	P	P	P	P
2.	Reinforced masonry wall, half height (4' high)	P		P	P	P
3.	Unreinforced masonry wall, full height	P	P	P	P	P
4.	Unreinforced masonry wall, half height	P		P	P	P
5.	3/4" drywall, full height, studs 16" apart	P/T	P/T	P/T	P/T	P/T
6.	3/4" drywall, half height, studs 16" apart	P/T	T	P/T	P/T	P/T-
7.	3/4" plywood, full height, studs 16" apart	T	T	T	T	T
8.	3/4" plywood, half height, studs 16" apart	T		T	T	T

Table 4-2. Selected facility barrier materials

Barrier Function					
Selected Permanent and Temporary Barrier Materials	Establish Boundaries	Deter Unauthorized Entry	Detect with IDS or Surveillance Sensor Platform	Prevent Visual Observation	Channel Pedestrian and Vehicle Traffic
9. Safety glass panel	P/T				P/T
10. Ballistic-resistant glass panel	P				P
11. Acrylic panel	P/T			P	P
12. Polycarbonate panel	P				P
13. Glass-clad polycarbonate panel	P				P
14. Safety glass security grid, panels less than 10" diameter each	P	P		P	P
15. Ballistic-resistant glass security grid, panels less than 10" diameter each	P	P		P	P
16. Ballistic-resistant steel-ply panels, 16 gauge or better	P	P		P	P
17. Security grills	P	P	P-		
18. Security shutters, ballistic-resistant materials		P		P	

Legend :
IDS = intrusion detection system
P = permanent construction
T = temporary construction
A minus sign after the letter means that the material and construction techniques used in erecting a barrier for this purpose may not provide satisfactory security enhancements or may not be durable. Use of glass, acrylic, or polycarbonate materials to provide a visual screen requires use of translucent variants of these.

4-49. If permanent barrier materials are not readily available, expedient materials may be used. Table 4-3, page 4-14, shows a few of these materials and for which type of barrier they can be used.

Table 4-3. Selected expedient barrier materials

Selected Permanent and Temporary Barrier Materials	Barrier Function				
	Establish Boundaries	Deter Unauthorized Entry	Detect with IDS or Surveillance Sensor Platform	Prevent Visual Observation	Channel Pedestrian and Vehicle Traffic
1. Plastic sheeting	X			X	X
2. Canvas sheets, awnings	X			X	X
3. Plywood sheets	X	X	X	X	X
4. Acrylic panels	X	X		X	X
5. Polycarbonate panels	X				X
6. Safety tape	X				X
7. Rope	X				X
8. Chains	X	X			X
9. Safety barrels or empty oil drums	X		X		X
10. Traffic cones	X				X
11. Safety nets	X	X	X	X	X
12. Blast curtains				X	
13. Fire curtains				X	
14. Office furniture	X	X	X	X	X
15. Sandbags	X		X		X

Legend:
IDS   intrusion detection system

INSPECTION AND MAINTENANCE OF BARRIERS AND SECURITY SYSTEM COMPONENTS

4-50. Barriers should be checked routinely for defects that facilitate unauthorized entry, and such defects should be reported to supervisory personnel, engineer personnel, or to the director of public works. Inspections should consider the following maintenance problems that can have adverse implications for security.

- Damaged areas (cuts in fabric, broken posts).
- Deterioration (corrosion).
- Erosion of soil beneath the barrier.
- Loose fittings (barbed wire, outriggers, and fabric fasteners).
- Growth in the clear zones that afford cover for possible intruders.
- Obstructions that afford concealment or aid entry or exit for an intruder.
- Evidence of illegal or improper intrusion or attempted intrusion.
- Unauthorized construction that might facilitate access.

Chapter 5

Security Lighting

The primary focus of this chapter is on exterior security lighting. Specific requirements for Army security lighting are described in AR 50-5 for nuclear weapons, AR 190-11 for AA&E, AR 190-51 for Army property at unit and installation level, and AR 190-59 for chemical agents. Other key publications for security lighting include TM 5-811-1 and UFC 3-530-01. Good protective lighting is achieved by adequate, even light on bordering areas, glaring light in the eyes of the intruder, and relatively little light on security personnel and security patrol routes. In addition to seeing long distances, security forces must be able to see low contrasts, such as indistinct outlines of silhouettes, and be able to spot an intruder who may be exposed to view for only a few seconds. Higher levels of brightness improve all of these abilities. Security lighting should—

- Discourage or deter attempts at entry by intruders. Proper illumination may lead a potential intruder to believe detection is inevitable.
- Make detection likely if entry is attempted.
- Prevent glare that may temporarily blind the guards.
- Be designed and used in a manner that does not impede the use of closed-circuit television (CCTV) systems or other automated monitoring systems.

PRINCIPLES OF SECURITY LIGHTING

5-1.   Security lighting is a psychological deterrent and should be installed along perimeter fences to aid with continuous or periodic observation; however, security lighting should not be used as a psychological deterrent alone.

5-2.   Security lighting is desirable for those sensitive areas or structures within the perimeter that are under observation. Such areas or structures include pier and dock areas, vital buildings, storage areas, motor pools, and vulnerable control points in communication and power- and water-distribution systems. In interior areas where night operations are conducted, adequate lighting facilitates the detection of unauthorized persons approaching or attempting malicious acts within the area.

5-3.   Lighting should never be used alone but rather in conjunction with other security measures, such as fixed security posts, patrols, fences, and ESS. In planning protective lighting, high-brightness contrast between intruder and background should be the first consideration. In addition to seeing long distances, security forces must be able to see low contrasts (such as indistinct outlines of silhouettes). Higher levels of illumination improve these abilities.

5-4.   The volume and intensity of lighting will vary with the surfaces to be illuminated. Dark, dirty surfaces or surfaces painted with camouflage paint require more illumination than installations and buildings with clean concrete, light brick, or glass surfaces. Rough, uneven terrain with dense underbrush requires more illumination to achieve a constant level of brightness than do manicured lawns.

5-5.   When the same amount of light falls on an object and its background, the observer must depend on contrasts in the amount of light reflected. His ability to distinguish poor contrasts is significantly improved by increasing the illumination level. The observer primarily sees an outline or a silhouette when the intruder is darker than his background. Using light finishes on the lower parts of buildings and structures may expose an intruder who depends on dark clothing and darkened face and hands. Stripes on walls have also been used effectively, as they provide recognizable breaks in outlines or silhouettes. Providing broad-lighted areas (against which intruders can be seen) around and in the installation can also create good observation conditions.

5-6. Security lighting enables guard-force personnel—while minimizing their presence—to observe activities around or inside an installation. An adequate level of illumination for all approaches to an installation will not discourage unauthorized entry; however, adequate lighting improves the ability of security personnel to assess visually and intervene on attempts at unauthorized entry.

5-7. To be effective, two basic systems or a combination of both may be used to provide practical and effective security lighting. The first method is to light the boundaries and approaches; the second is to light the area and structures within the property's general boundaries.

5-8. The four categories or types of lighting units used for security lighting systems include—

- **Continuous lighting.** Continuous lighting (stationary luminary) is the most common security-lighting system. It consists of a series of fixed lights arranged to flood a given area continuously during darkness with overlapping cones of light. When continuous lighting is not cost effective, motion-detection lighting should be considered. Three primary methods of using continuous lighting are glare projection, controlled lighting, and surface lighting.
    - Glare projection consist of lamps mounted on poles inside a protected area and directed outward. This method is used when the glare of lights directed across the surrounding area will not be annoying, nor will it interfere with adjacent operations. Glare projection is a strong deterrent to a potential intruder because it makes it difficult to see inside the area. Guards are protected by being kept in comparative darkness and able to observe the area.
    - Controlled lighting consists of lamps mounted on 30-foot poles and shines down and out. This lighting is most effective when it limits the width of the lighted strip outside the perimeter, such as along highways.
    - Surface lighting consists of lamps mounted at ground surface and shines in and up onto the surface of a building or structure. Surface lighting illuminates the face of a building from the ground up and assists the security force by elongating or exaggerating the shadow of an intruder who approaches a building.
- **Standby lighting.** Standby lighting has a layout similar to continuous lighting. However, the luminaries are not continuously lit but are either automatically or manually turned on when suspicious activity is detected or suspected by the security force or alarm systems. Motion-activated lighting is one automatic method that can be used to deter intruders and draw attention to an area where an intruder has tripped a motion-activated light.
- **Movable or portable lighting.** Movable lighting consists of manually operated, movable searchlights that may be lit during hours of darkness or only as needed. The system normally is used to supplement continuous or standby lighting.
- **Emergency lighting.** Emergency lighting is a system of lighting that may duplicate any or all of the above systems. Its use is limited to times of power failure or other emergencies that render the normal system inoperative. It depends on an alternative power source, such as installed or portable generators or batteries. Emergency lighting systems should be protected against unauthorized access and use.

PLANNING CONSIDERATIONS

5-9. Security lighting requirements should be identified, justified, and funded separate from operational lighting requirements. The designated provost marshal or PSO should play a key role in providing guidance for security lighting requirements. High-quality lighting depends on the following factors:

- Lighting function.
- Luminance.
- Uniformity.
- Glare.
- Light trespass.
- Color rendition.
- Energy efficiency.

LIGHTING FUNCTION

5-10. Lighting function refers to the purpose of the lighting under consideration. Often lighting designed for security will provide additional lighting functions. How well it performs these functions will depend on how well the lighting plan was designed. The more the lighting function is considered in the initial planning phase, the greater the probability that additional functional goals will be met.

5-11. Security lighting usually requires less intensity than working lights, except for identification and inspection at ACPs. Each area of a facility presents its own unique set of considerations based on physical layout, terrain, atmospheric and climatic conditions, and security requirements. Information is available from the manufacturers of lighting equipment and from the installation's director of public works, who will assist in designing a lighting system. This information includes—

- Descriptions, characteristics, and specifications of various lighting fixtures, arc, and gaseous-discharge lamps.
- Lighting patterns of various fixtures.
- Typical layouts showing the most efficient height and spacing of equipment.
- Minimum levels of illumination and lighting uniformity required for various applications.
- Protection of the lighting system by locating the system inside barriers. Install protective covers or cages over lamps, mount them on high poles, protect switch boxes, and bury power lines.
- Installation of motion-activated lighting.
- Installation of photoelectric cells to turn lights on and off automatically.
- Restrictions of light installation in the vicinity of navigable waters and air operations.

LUMINANCE

5-12. Luminance is the measurement of light existing in a given area or at a selected point in that area. Illuminance is a measure of the amount of light falling on a surface; it is measured in output of light (lumens) compared to power input (watts) to define lamp efficiency (efficacy). Lamp output (lumens per watt) is measured when the lamp is new.

5-13. Illuminance is measured in two ways: the English measurement, which is foot-candles, or the metric unit, which is lux. One foot-candle is the illuminance at a point on a surface that is 1 foot from, and perpendicular to, a uniform point source of one candela. One lux is the illuminance at the same point at a distance of 1 meter from the source. One foot-candle equals 10.76 lux. (For example, 50 foot-candles equals 538 lux.)

5-14. There are commercially made light meters available to measure illuminance. Older model light meters indicate in units of foot-candles, while newer models indicate in units of lux.

5-15. When planning for security lighting, remember the direction that the light is coming from (horizontally or vertically) and that the condition of the light fixtures (new or maintained) must be considered. Table 5-1, page 5-4, shows the lighting recommendations for specific areas in foot-candles and lux (lux factors have been rounded down). These lighting recommendations comply with the Illuminating Engineering Society of North America (IESNA) standards for similar areas and facilities; however, they are merely general guidelines. Lighting levels above those indicated in table 5-1 may be appropriate where practical and desired. For example, it may be necessary to provide additional task lighting in the identification and inspection areas to support adequate identification of vehicle occupants and contents. Standards should be established based on the particular needs of the facility user and the security force.

Table 5-1. Lux and foot-candle values

Areas	Foot-Candles	Lux
ACP		
Approach zone and response zone	3	32
Parking and roadways	3	32
Access control zone	5	53
Search areas (vehicle and ID checking)	10	107
Vital locations or structures	5	53
Building surrounds	1	10
Buildings Floodlighted		
Bright surroundings		
Light surfaces	15	161
Medium-light surfaces	20	215
Medium-dark surfaces	30	322
Dark surfaces	50	538
Dark surroundings		
Light surfaces	5	53
Medium-light surfaces	10	107
Medium-dark surfaces	15	161
Dark surfaces	20	215
Gates and doors	2	21
Office space	50	538
Parking Areas (Other Than ACP)		
Self-parking	1	10
Attendant parking	2	21
Covered parking	5	53
Rail Yards, Marshaling, and Loading Areas		
Loading and unloading platforms	20	215
Freight car interiors	10	107
Lumber yards	1	10
Piers		
Freight	20	215
Passenger	20	215
Active shipping area surrounds	5	53
Service Station (At Grade)		
Light surroundings		
Approach	3	32
Driveway	5	53

Table 5-1. Lux and foot-candle values

Areas	Foot-Candles	Lux
Pump island	30	322
Building faces	30	322
Service areas	7	75
Landscape highlights	5	53
Dark surroundings		
Approach	1.5	16
Driveway	1.5	16
Pump island	20	215
Building faces	10	107
Service areas	3	32
Landscape highlights	2	21
Ship Yards		
General	5	53
Ways	10	107
Fabrication areas	30	322
Storage Yards		
Active	20	215
Inactive	1	10
Legend: ACP access control point ID identification		

5-16. Limited and exclusion areas. Specific requirements for Army security lighting are described in AR 50-5 for nuclear weapons, AR 190-11 for AA&E, AR 190-51 for Army property at unit and installation level, and AR 190-59 for chemical agents. Security lighting applications that include CCTV cameras for controlled areas should be under the control of the guard force. For critical areas (such as weapons storage), instantaneous lighting with a backup source is required. Any period without lighting in a critical area is unacceptable. Therefore, these areas generally have a requirement for backup power.

UNIFORMITY

5-17. Lighting uniformity means that light is provided in areas that are traveled by security personnel in such a way that they can see ahead and to the sides with an absence of dark areas caused by shadows. The lighting should be brightest in the secure area, with the light gradually less in the areas adjacent to the high-illumination areas.

GLARE

5-18. In most exterior applications, security is best achieved by reducing glare. In some circumstances, such as at entries and checkpoints, glare can be used to increase vertical illuminance on approaching vehicles or individuals, while increasing visibility for guards and patrols. Glare occurs when a bright light source is seen against a dark background. There are a number of factors that must be considered when designing a secure facility to use glare to enhance security. These factors are—

- Where will the light be placed?
- What are the typical angles of view?
- What type of lamp and luminaire (lighting fixture) will be used?
- What is the mounting height of the light?

LIGHT TRESPASS

5-19. Light trespass is when light from one facility spills over into an adjoining facility, where it could cause interference with the security of that area. The factors that affect glare are also a consideration for light trespass.

COLOR RENDITION

5-20. Because different light sources radiate more in one area of the color spectrum than others (chromaticity or whiteness of light—see table 5-2), certain colors will be emphasized more than others when they illuminate a neutral surface. This color shift can cause problems with identifying persons and objects in the lighted area. It is therefore important, when planning the site lighting, that the type of light elements be matched to the required task. Table 5-2 provides the color rendition of the most frequently used lamps.

Table 5-2. Lamp chromaticity and color rendition

Type of Lamp	Color of Light	Use	Color Rendition
Incandescent	Standard for daylight.	Exterior and interior locations where color recognition and human appearance are important.	Good color rendition.
Fluorescent	Excellent daylight color rendition.		
Tungsten-halogen			
Mercury vapor	Good daylight color rendition heavy on the blue side.		
Metal halide	Closest to daylight.	Exterior and interior locations and CCTV where color recognition and human appearance are important.	
High-pressure sodium	Golden-white to yellow.	Exterior locations	Reds appear brown.
Low-pressure sodium	In the yellow range.	Suited for use where color recognition and human appearance are of no importance. Exterior and interior locations. Good for black and white surveillance systems.	All colors appear as shades of yellow grey.
Legend: CCTV closed-circuit television			

ENERGY EFFICIENCY

5-21. Lamp efficiency (efficacy) is measured in terms of lumens (light output) per watt (power required to operate the lamp). Efficacy refers to the amount of light (lumens) that is produced by a light source for every watt of energy. Different light sources produce light at different efficacies. Incandescent lamps have the lowest efficacy, whereas fluorescent, induction, and metal halide sources have the highest efficacies. Efficacy must be considered along with the application to select the most efficacious source that will light the surface or task appropriately.

5-22. The careful selection of light sources to use the most efficient and lowest-wattage light source for the application reduces energy use and cost. This results in a significant benefit with a low-cost increase. For example, fluorescent lamps, typically rated in milliamperes (MA), may have an initial higher cost; however, they are more efficient, have a longer life, and typically pay back in energy savings and replacement costs in a few years.

5-23. The efficacies of the basic lamp families are shown in table 5-3.

Table 5-3. Efficacies of basic lamp families

Type of Lamp	Wattage Range	Initial Lumens Per Watt Including Ballast Losses	Average Rated Life (Hours)
Low-pressure sodium	18–180	62–150	12,000–18,000
High-pressure sodium	35–1,000	51–130	7,500–24,000+
Metal halide	70–2,000	69–115	5,000–20,000
Mercury Vapor			
Standard	40–1,000	24–60	12,000–24,000+
Self-ballasted	160–1,250	14–25	12,000–20,000
Fluorescent	4–215	14–95	6,000–20,000+
Incandescent	15–1,500	8–24	750–3,500
Tungsten-halogen	20–1,875	10–30	950–6,000

5-24. Lamp efficiency degrades over time—with the amount of energy consumed remaining constant—while the light output slowly reduces. This is called lamp lumen depreciation. The light of low-pressure sodium lamps remains constant throughout their lives. However, their energy consumption goes up, making them become less efficient. In the planning of security lighting for a site, the cost of operation of older lamps must be weighed versus the cost of lamp replacement.

5-25. In planning a security lighting system, the PSO must consider the following:

- Cost of replacing lamps and cleaning fixtures, as well as the cost of providing the required equipment (such as ladders and mechanical buckets) to perform this maintenance.
- Provision of manual-override capability during a blackout, including photoelectric controls. These controls may be desirable in a peacetime situation but undesirable when a mandatory blackout is a possibility.
- Effects of local weather conditions on lighting systems.
- Fluctuating or erratic voltages in the primary power source.
- Grounding requirements.
- Provisions for rapid lamp replacement.
- Lamp compatibility with the luminaire.
- Use of lighting to support a CCTV system.
- Lighting requirements for adjoining properties and activities.
- Strike or warm-up time of the lamp (the time required before the light will function properly when first turned on). See table 5-4, page 5-8, for warm-up times.
- Restrike time of the lamp (the time required before the light will function properly after a brief power interruption).
- Color accuracy.
- Other facilities requiring lighting, such as parking areas.

Table 5-4. Warm-up and restrike time for lamp families

Type of Lamp	Warm-Up Time	Restrike Time
Low-pressure sodium	2–5 minutes	1–2 minutes
High-pressure sodium	2–5 minutes	1–2 minutes
Metal halide	2–5 minutes	10–15 minutes

Table 5-4. Warm-up and restrike time for lamp families

Type of Lamp	Warm-Up Time	Restrike Time
Mercury vapor	5–10 minutes	2–10 minutes
Fluorescent	1– 2 minutes	1– 2 minutes
Incandescent	Instant on	Instant on
Tungsten-halogen	Instant on	Instant on

TYPES OF LIGHTING UNITS (LUMINAIRES)

5-26. A luminaire is a complete lighting unit, including lamps, ballast(s), and lens; the units come in all sizes and shapes, and their use depends on the installation's overall security requirements. A lamp's compatibility with a luminaire is important when luminaire selections are restricted. This sometimes is the case in modernization projects when existing fixtures are reused for purposes of economy. Existing luminaires can be converted to accept a new kind of lamp; this will entail the installation of new ballasts. It may be more cost-effective to replace the luminaires rather than use the old ones.

POLES AND MOUNTS

5-27. Some outdoor lighting fixtures are mounted directly into the ground or may be somewhat decorative in nature and strung through a tree or shrubbery. In the lighting of an area, however, height is essential and will have an impact on the lighting design, specifications, and the system used. See figure 5-1 and table 5-5 for the types of luminaires, their uses, beam coverage, and pole heights.

5-28. Increased height permits use of higher-wattage, more efficient lamps and luminaires, resulting in reduced glare. Additionally, more than one luminaire can be mounted on the taller poles. With more lights per pole, fewer poles will be needed. In a decision on the types of poles or mounts to be used, the overall design configuration of the site must be considered.

5-29. Pole height is not the only issue; the composition of the pole and mechanical design are also factors that impact the use of the pole. Pole selection factors include—

- Initial cost.
- Maintenance requirements.
- Durability.
- Aesthetics.
- Pole design either supporting or impeding maintenance.
- Pole placement for proper illumination with minimum operational impact.

5-30. The poles should be designed, when considering maintenance, so that the luminaires are easy to access and maintain. If in-house maintenance is performed, any special maintenance equipment will need to be on hand.

5-31. In many instances, poles will not be needed, because the luminaires can be mounted on the sides or roofs of buildings or other facilities in the complex.

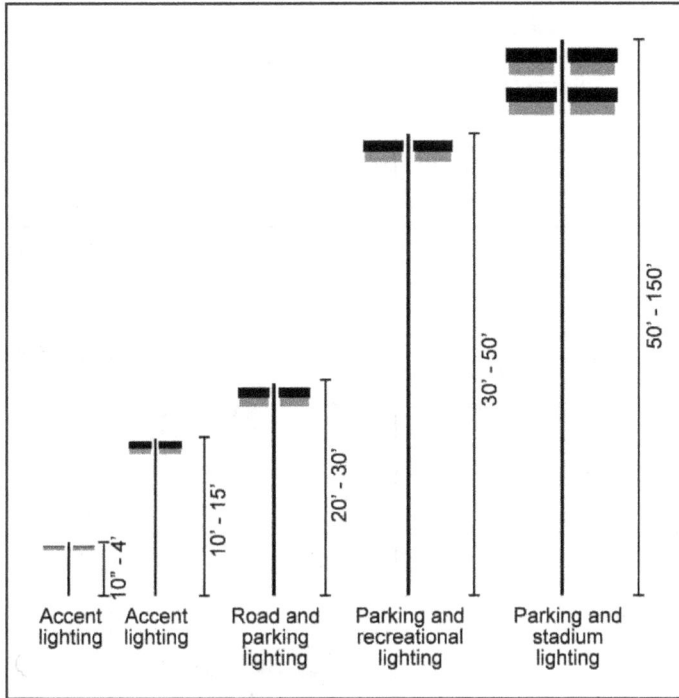

Figure 5-1. Poles and mounts

Table 5-5. Luminaire use and light coverage

Luminaire Type	Example	Light Pattern	Description of Use and Pole Heights
Cutoff			This luminaire is used to reduce direct glare in lighting medium-to-large areas where control of spill light and direct glare is important. Example is in parking lots next to residential areas. Pole heights can vary from 30 to 50 feet.
Refractor			This luminaire is used for highway, street, and general-area lighting where spill lighting and glare control are less important. Pole heights are 50 feet and up.
Low-mounted site lighting			This low-wattage luminaire is used around buildings where aesthetic appeal is needed. It produces

Table 5-5. Luminaire use and light coverage

Luminaire Type	Example	Light Pattern	Description of Use and Pole Heights
			low-level, glare-free lighting of small areas. Pole heights are 4 feet and under.
Post-top (uncontrolled)			This low-wattage luminaire is used for decorative purposes and provides 360 degrees of light distribution. A considerable amount of light is lost above the horizontal. Pole heights are from 4 to 10 feet, depending on the area design.
Post-top (controlled)			This low-to-medium-wattage luminaire is used for site lighting for medium-to-small areas and pedestrian walkways. It directs most of the light into the desired area. Pole heights are from 4 to 10 feet, depending on the area design.
High-mast			This is a high-wattage luminaire used for large-area coverage with good glare control. It is pole-mounted and ranges from 60 to 150 feet high. Areas of use are railroad yards, large parking lots, industrial yards, and highway interchanges.
Floodlight or projector (full cutoff)			This medium-to-high-wattage luminaire is used to control glare and light trespass. The shape of the luminaire allows a sharp cutoff of the upper light beam. This luminaire is used on airport aprons and areas adjacent to residential neighborhoods. Pole heights are up to 50 feet.

Table 5-5. Luminaire use and light coverage

Luminaire Type	Example	Light Pattern	Description of Use and Pole Heights
Floodlight or projector (semicutoff)			This medium-to-high-wattage luminaire is used to control spill light and glare with louvers and hoods. This luminaire is typically used near residential areas. Pole heights are up to 50 feet.
Floodlight or projector (noncutoff)			This medium-to-high-wattage luminaire is used to provide a tight symmetrical beam. It is used for buildings, sports, and area lighting where light spillage is not a concern. Mounting height will depend on the application—e.g., the height of the building will dictate how high the luminaire can be mounted or, for sports, the pole can be from 60 to 150 feet.
Building-mounted (cutoff type)			This is a low-wattage luminaire used for tighter beam control and low brightness. It is used to control light spillage/trespass and glare. It is used on all types of buildings. Mounting height depends on the building height and the desired coverage area.
Building-mounted (refractor-type)			This is a low-wattage luminaire used to produce a wide-beam distribution. It is used for general lighting of buildings, and the glare may be objectionable. Mounting height depends on the building height.

FENCED PERIMETERS

5-32. Fenced perimeters require the lighting specifications indicated in UFC 4-020-02. Specific lighting requirements are based on whether the perimeter is isolated, semi-isolated, or nonisolated (see figure 5-2).

- Isolated fenced perimeters are fence lines around areas where the fence is 100 feet or more from buildings or operating areas. The approach area is clear of obstruction for 100 or more feet outside of the fence. Other personnel do not use the area. Use glare projection for these perimeters, and keep patrol routes unlit.

- Semi-isolated fenced perimeters are fence lines where approach areas are clear of obstruction for 60 to 100 feet outside of the fence. The general public or installation personnel seldom have reason to be in the area. Use controlled lighting for these perimeters and keep patrol routes in relative darkness.

- Nonisolated fenced perimeters are fence lines immediately adjacent to operating areas. These areas may be in an installation or public thoroughfares. Outsiders or installation personnel may move about freely in this approach area. The width of the lighted strip depends on the clear zones inside and outside the fence. Use controlled lighting for these perimeters. It may not be practical to keep the patrol area dark.

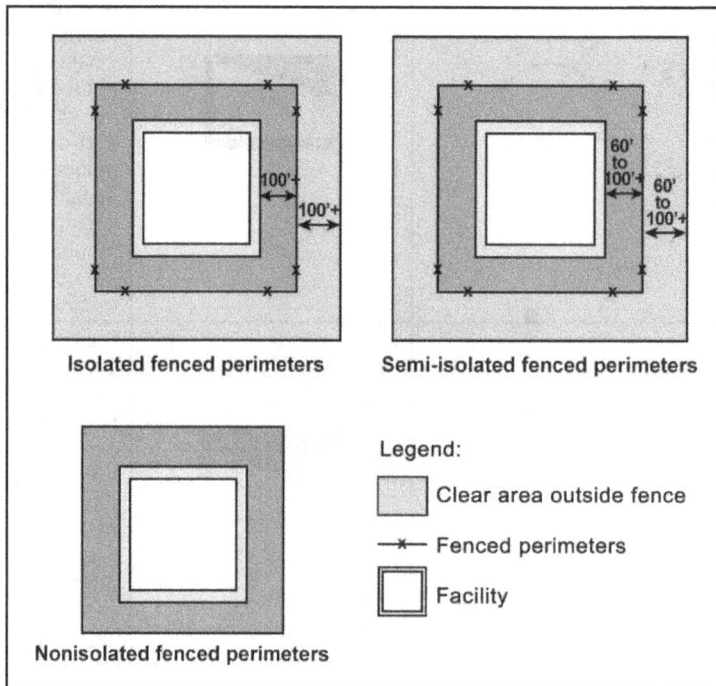

Figure 5-2. Isolated, semi-isolated, and nonisolated perimeters

ENTRANCES

5-33. Entrances for pedestrians should have two or more lighting units that provide adequate illumination for recognition of persons and examination of credentials. Vehicle access points should have two lighting units located to facilitate the complete inspection of passenger cars, trucks, and freight cars, as well as their contents and passengers. Semiactive and inactive entrances should have the same degree of continuous lighting as the remainder of the perimeter, with standby lighting to be used when the entrance becomes active. Gatehouses at entrances should have a low level of interior illumination, enabling guards to see approaching pedestrians and vehicles.

OTHER AREAS

5-34. Areas and structures within the property line of the installation consist of yards; storage spaces; large, open working areas; piers; docks; and other sensitive areas and structures. Guidelines for applying security lighting to these areas and structures include—

- Open yards (unoccupied land only) and outdoor storage spaces (material storage areas, railroad sidings, motor pools, and parking areas) should be illuminated. An open yard adjacent to a perimeter (between guards and fences) will be illuminated according to the perimeter's illumination requirements. Where lighting is necessary in other open yards, illumination will not be less than 0.2 foot-candles at any point.
- Lighting units should be placed in outdoor storage spaces to provide an adequate distribution of light in aisles, passageways, and recesses to eliminate shadowed areas where unauthorized persons may hide.
- Illuminating both water approaches and the pier area safeguards piers and docks located on an installation. Decks on open piers will be illuminated to at least 1 foot-candle, and the water approaches (extending to a distance of 100 feet from the pier) to at least 0.5 foot-candles. The area beneath the pier floor will be lit with small-wattage floodlights arranged on the piling. Movable lighting is recommended as a part of the protective lighting system for piers and docks. The lighting must not in any way violate marine rules and regulations (for example, it must not be glaring to pilots). Consult the United States Coast Guard for approval of protective lighting adjacent to navigable waters.
- Illuminating airports or airfields must not in any way violate Federal Aviation Administration (FAA) rules and regulations (for example, lighting must not be glaring to pilots). Consult the FAA for approval of protective lighting on or adjacent to airports and airfields.

WIRING SYSTEMS

5-35. Both parallel and series circuits may be used to advantage in protective lighting systems, depending on the type of luminary used and other design features of the system. The circuit should be arranged so that failure of any one lamp shall not leave a large portion of the perimeter line or a major segment of a critical or vulnerable position in darkness. Connection should be such that normal interruptions caused by overloads, industrial accidents, and building or brush fires shall not interrupt the protective system. In addition, feeder lines should be located underground (or sufficiently inside the perimeter, in the case of overhead wiring) to minimize the possibility of sabotage or vandalism from outside the perimeter. Another advantage to underground wiring is reduced effects from adverse weather conditions.

5-36. The design should provide for simplicity and economy in system maintenance and should require a minimum of shutdowns for routine repairs, cleaning, and lamp replacement. It is necessary in some instances to install a duplicate wiring system.

5-37. Periodic inspections should be made of all electrical circuits to replace or repair worn parts, tighten connections, and check insulation. Keep fixtures clean and properly aimed.

POWER SOURCES

5-38. A secure auxiliary power source (generator and battery backup) and power-distribution system for the facility should be installed to provide redundancy to critical security lighting and other security equipment. During expeditionary operations, primary power may not exist or may be subject to constraints or interruptions that are due to poor infrastructure or hostile activity. Auxiliary power sources must be available for critical electrical loads and must be secured against direct and indirect fires as well as sabotage. If automatic-transfer switches are not installed, security procedures must designate the responsibility for the manual start of the source.

5-39. Primary and alternate power sources must be identified. The following is a partial list of considerations:

- The primary source is usually a local public utility.
- An alternate source (standby batteries or diesel fuel-driven generators may be used) is provided where required and should—
  - Start automatically upon failure of primary power.
  - Be adequate to power the entire lighting system.
  - Be equipped with adequate fuel storage and supply.
  - Be tested under load to ensure efficiency and effectiveness.
  - Be located in a controlled area for additional security.

5-40. Under ideal circumstances, power supplies related to physical security systems should be routed to the installation separate from other utility services. In addition, power supplies for physical security systems should enter each protected facility, as well as each protected enclave or restricted area within a facility, separate from other power and utility services.

5-41. System controls and switches for protective lighting systems should be inside the protected area and locked or guarded at all times. An alternative is to locate controls in a central station similar to, or as a part of, the system used in intrusion-detection alarm central monitoring stations. High-impact plastic shields may be installed over lights to prevent destruction by thrown objects or other means.

CLOSED-CIRCUIT TELEVISION AND CAMERA LIGHTING CONSIDERATIONS

5-42. When CCTV is used as part of the security operation, it is important to coordinate the lighting and CCTV system. The lighting system for CCTV must be designed so that, under normal operating conditions, the lighting is balanced to provide the best image contrast possible. Standard CCTV can provide images from normal daylight to twilight conditions. Under other-than-normal operating conditions, artificial lighting must be provided. When an area is being lighted, the range of foot-candles should not exceed 6 and not be less than 2.

5-43. TM 5-811-1 provides further information on designing lighting systems for use with CCTV. The following considerations apply when lighting systems are intended to support CCTV assessment or surveillance:

- Camera's field of view.
- Lighting intensity levels.
- Maximum light-to-dark ratio.
- Scene reflectance.
- Daylight-to-darkness transitions.
- Camera mounting systems relative to the lighting source.
- Camera's spectral response.
- Luminaire cold-start time.
- Luminaire restrike time.

Chapter 6

Electronic Security System

The ESS consists of ACS (card reader systems, electronic entry systems, and various subsystems); IDS; CCTV systems (including both video motion detection and intelligent video systems); data-transmission media (DTM) systems; and alarm reporting systems for monitoring, controlling, and displaying various alarm system information. ESSs are an important component of the overall physical protection plan. To establish the ESS requirements, a planning team such as the protection working group uses the process in UFC 4-020-01 to identify the design criteria—which include the assets to be protected, the threats to those assets, and the levels of protection to be provided for the assets against the identified threats. The planning team generally consists of the facility user, antiterrorism officer, operations officer, security, logistics, and engineers. Army Service Component Commands are designated as approval authority for nonstandard physical security equipment procurement procedures. AR 190-11, AR 190-13, AR 190-51, UFC 4-020-04A, UFC 4-021-02NF and UFGS 13720A provide guidance to commanders, designers, and engineers on how to design, install, operate, and maintain ESSs for projects, to include new construction, additions, renovations, expeditionary, or temporary construction.

ELECTRONIC SECURITY SYSTEM CHARACTERISTICS

6-1.   For effective intrusion protection, the ESS should operate on detect, delay, and respond principles. The installation PSO assesses security force response capabilities and advises the planning team of reaction times. The system should be designed to ensure that the time between detection of an intrusion and response by security forces is less than the time it takes for damage or compromise of assets to occur. Depending on the category of the asset, there may be dictated response times. For example, a response time of no more than 15 minutes is required for designated members of the response force at a chemical agent storage facility (see AR 190-59). The primary focus of the PSO is to ensure that the needs of the security/response force are met and that security personnel are thoroughly trained on the various ESSs.

6-2.   When an intruder is attempting to penetrate—or has penetrated—a protected area, the basic function of an ESS is to notify security personnel in sufficient time to allow the response force to intercept and apprehend the intruder. The exterior and interior systems should be configured as layers of unbroken rings concentrically surrounding the asset. These rings should correspond to defensive layers that constitute the delay system. The first detection layer is located at the outermost defensive layer necessary to provide the required delay.

6-3.   To allow the response force time to apprehend the intruder, there must be sufficient physical delay between the point where the intruder is first detected and his objective. The delay time must be equal to or greater than the response time (refer to UFC 4-020-01). The total delay time is defined as the sum of all of the delay times of the barriers, the time required to cross the areas between barriers after an intrusion alarm has been reported, and the time required to compromise the asset and leave.

6-4.   For an ESS, the response time is defined as the time it takes the security force to arrive at the scene after an initial alarm is received at the security center. Detection at the perimeter increases the response time, as opposed to detection at the interior wall of the critical asset.

ACCESS CONTROL SYSTEMS

6-5. ACSs ensure that only authorized personnel gain access to controlled areas. These systems consist of electronic locks, card readers, biometric readers, alarms, and computer systems to monitor and control access. An ACS compares an individual's credential against a verified database. If the information is verified, the system sends output signals that allow authorized personnel to pass through controlled portals such as gates or doors (UFC 4-021-02NF).

6-6. ACS locks are normally used for access control only and should be backed up by door deadbolt locking devices when a facility is unoccupied. These types of locking devices may be used on nonsensitive administrative facilities as exterior locking devices, provided that they fall to a secure position when electrical power is removed.

6-7. ACSs typically have the capability to log and archive entry attempts. These systems are normally integrated with other ESS, such as IDS and CCTV systems. Signals from the ACS are communicated to the security center through the transmission lines of the DTM. Electronic ACSs are reliable, provide a high level of security, and reduce manpower requirements.

6-8. ACS entry-authorization identifiers are grouped into three categories:
- Credential devices.
- Coded devices.
- Biometric devices.

CREDENTIAL DEVICES

6-9. A credential device identifies a person having legitimate authority to enter a controlled area. A coded credential (plastic card or key) contains a prerecorded, machine-readable code. An electric signal unlocks the door if the prerecorded code matches the code stored in the system when the card is read. Credential devices only authenticate the credential, assuming that a user with an acceptable credential is authorized to enter. Various technologies are used to store the code on or within a card. The most commonly used types of cards are described below.

Magnetic-Stripe Card

6-10. A stripe of magnetic material located along one edge of the card is encoded with data (sometimes encrypted). The data is read by moving the card past a magnetic read head.

Proximity Card

6-11. A proximity card is not physically inserted into a reader; the coded pattern on the card is sensed when it is brought within several inches of the reader. Several techniques are used to code cards. One technique uses a number of electrically tuned circuits embedded in the card. Data are encoded by varying resonant frequencies of the tuned circuits. The reader contains a transmitter that continually sweeps through a specified range of frequencies and a receiver that senses the pattern of resonant frequencies contained in the card. Another technique uses an integrated circuit embedded in the card to generate a code that can be magnetically or electrostatically coupled to the reader. The power required to activate embedded circuitry can be provided by a small battery embedded in the card or by magnetically coupling power from the reader.

Smart Card

6-12. A smart card is embedded with a microprocessor, memory, communication circuitry, and a battery. The card contains edge contacts that enable a reader to communicate with the microprocessor. Entry-control information and other data may be stored in the memory of the microprocessor. The federal standard for electronic smart cards is described in the Federal Information Processing Standards (FIPS) 201-1.

Bar Code

6-13. A bar code consists of black bars printed on white paper or tape that can be easily read with an optical scanner. This type of coding is not widely used for entry-control applications because it can be easily duplicated. It is possible to conceal the code by applying an opaque mask over it. In this approach, an IR scanner is used to interpret the printed code. For low-level security areas, the use of bar codes can provide a cost-effective solution for access control. Coded strips and opaque masks can be attached to existing identification badges, alleviating the need for complete badge replacement.

CODED DEVICES

6-14. Coded devices operate on the principle that a person has been issued a code to enter into an entry-control device. This code will match the code stored in the device and permit entry. Depending on the application, all persons authorized to enter the controlled area can use a single code or each authorized person can be assigned a unique code. Group codes are useful when the group is small and controls are primarily for keeping out the general public. Individual codes are usually required for control of entry to more critical areas. Coded devices verify the entered code's authenticity, and any person entering a correct code is authorized to enter the controlled area. Electronically coded devices include electronic and computer-controlled keypads.

Electronic Keypad Devices

6-15. The common telephone keypad (12 keys) is an example of an electronic keypad. This type of keypad consists of simple push-button switches that, when depressed, are decoded by digital logic circuits. When the correct sequence of buttons is pushed, an electronic signal unlocks the door for a few seconds.

Computer-Controlled Keypad Devices

6-16. These devices are similar to electronic keypad devices, except they are equipped with a microprocessor in the keypad or in a separate enclosure at a different location. The microprocessor monitors the sequence in which the keys are depressed and may provide additional functions, such as personal identification and digit scrambling. When the correct code is entered and all conditions are satisfied, an electronic signal unlocks the door.

BIOMETRIC DEVICES

6-17. The third basic technique used to control entry is based on the measurement of one or more physical or personal characteristics of an individual. Because most entry-control devices based on this technique rely on measurements of biological characteristics, they have become commonly known as biometric devices. These biometric devices continue to evolve, providing a greater degree of identification. Characteristics such as fingerprints, hand geometry, voiceprints, handwriting, and retinal blood-vessel patterns have been used for controlling entry. Typically, in enrolling individuals, several reference measurements are made of the selected characteristic and then stored in the device's memory or on a card. From then on, when that person attempts entry, a scan of the characteristic is compared with the reference data template. If a match is found, entry is granted. Rather than verifying an artifact, such as a code or a credential, biometric devices verify a person's physical characteristic, thus providing a form of identity verification. Because of personal physical characteristic verification, biometric devices are sometimes referred to as personnel identity-verification devices. The most commonly used biometric devices are described below.

Fingerprints

6-18. Fingerprint-verification devices use one of two approaches. One is pattern recognition of the whorls, loops, and tilts of the referenced fingerprint, which is stored in a digitized representation of the image and compared with the fingerprint of the prospective entrant. The second approach is minutiae comparison, which means that the endings and branching points of ridges and valleys of the referenced fingerprint are compared with the fingerprint of the prospective entrant.

Hand Geometry

6-19. Several devices are available that use hand geometry for personnel verification. These devices use a variety of physical measurements of the hand, such as finger length, finger curvature, hand width, webbing between fingers, and light transmissivity through the skin to verify identity. These devices are available in two- and three-dimensional units.

Retinal Patterns

6-20. This type of technique is based on the premise that the pattern of blood vessels on the retina of the human eye is unique to an individual. While the eye is focused on a visual target, a low-intensity IR light beam scans a circular area of the retina. The amount of light reflected from the eye is recorded as the beam progresses around the circular path. Reflected light is modulated by the difference in reflectivity between blood-vessel pattern and adjacent tissue. This information is processed and converted to a digital template that is stored as the signature of the eye. Contact lenses may be worn during the making of a retinal pattern device; however, glasses must be removed to preclude an inaccurate recording.

Device Combinations

6-21. Frequently, an automated entry-control system uses combinations of the three types of entry-control devices. Combining two different devices can significantly enhance the security level of the system and sometimes may reduce verification times.

INTRUSION DETECTION SYSTEMS

6-22. The function of an IDS is to detect intruders. The detection of an intruder starts the clock on the response timelines. The primary elements of the system include interior and exterior sensors, IDS central processing unit or local controllers, communications and interfaces with ACS, CCTV, and the security center. There are four types of IDS commonly used: local alarm, central station, police connection, and proprietary station.

6-23. Local alarm systems actuate a visible and/or audible signal, usually located on the exterior of the facility. Local alarms are simple alarm systems used for low-value assets. Response is generated from security forces located in the immediate area. Local alarms do not initiate the detect, delay, and respond sequence.

6-24. Central-station devices and circuits are automatically signaled to, recorded, maintained, and supervised from a central station with operators monitoring continuously. Normally, the security force monitors the signals and responds to any unauthorized entry into the protected area.

6-25. Direct-connection systems are transmitted to and annunciated at a local security or police dispatch center that records alarm annunciation. A formal agreement with local police may be required to ensure monitoring and response. Medical treatment facilities, base exchanges, commissaries, Reserve centers, or other facilities might benefit from this type of alarm system.

6-26. Proprietary-station systems are similar to central-station operation. This system is used throughout DOD installations, where security centers are owned, maintained, and staffed by DOD personnel who comprise the response force. The integrated commercial intrusion detection system (ICIDS) provides early warning of attempted actions against a protected asset by an intruder. The purpose of ICIDS is to monitor specially designated areas and facilities. When unauthorized attempts to enter these areas or facilities are detected, ICIDS provides an early-warning indication of intrusion attempts to a central monitoring location for operators to take required action. TM 5-6350-275-10 is the operator's manual for personnel responsible for operating and monitoring ICIDS.

6-27. IDS sensors are divided primarily into two groups, exterior sensors and interior sensors, depending on their environmental capability.

EXTERIOR SENSORS

6-28. Exterior sensors are designed to function in an outside environment. They provide excellent perimeter intrusion detection. Specific characteristics of exterior sensors include the following:

- Weatherproof.
- Less sensitive than interior sensors.
- Used for early detection of intruders along fences, walls, gates, and water or other land boundaries surrounding a protected structure.

6-29. Line sensors are exterior sensors that form an extended boundary through which intrusion can be detected. There are various categories of exterior sensors that include the following:

- Open-terrain sensors such as IR and microwave sensors.
- Property or fence-line sensors such as electromechanical systems and fiber-optic sensing systems.
- Other sensor technologies such as buried-cable and wide-area sensors.

Infrared Sensors

6-30. IR sensors are available in both active and passive models. An active sensor generates one or more near-IR beams that generate an alarm when interrupted. A passive sensor detects changes in thermal IR radiation from objects located within its field of view. Only active exterior IR sensors are used at Army facilities. Passive exterior sensors are not described here.

6-31. Active sensors consist of transmitter/receiver pairs. The transmitter contains an IR light source (such as a gallium arsenide light-emitting diode [LED] that generates an IR beam). The light source is usually modulated to reduce the sensor's susceptibility to unwanted alarms resulting from sunlight or other IR light sources. The receiver detects changes in the signal power of the received beam. To minimize nuisance alarms from birds or blowing debris, the alarm criteria usually require that a high percentage of the beam be blocked for a specific interval of time.

6-32. Active sensors can be single- or multiple-beam systems. Because single-beam sensors can be easily bypassed, multiple-beam systems are generally used in perimeter applications. There are two basic types of multiple-beam configurations: one type uses all transmitters on one post and all receivers on the other post; the second type uses one transmitter and several receivers on each post. Both types are illustrated in figure 6-1.

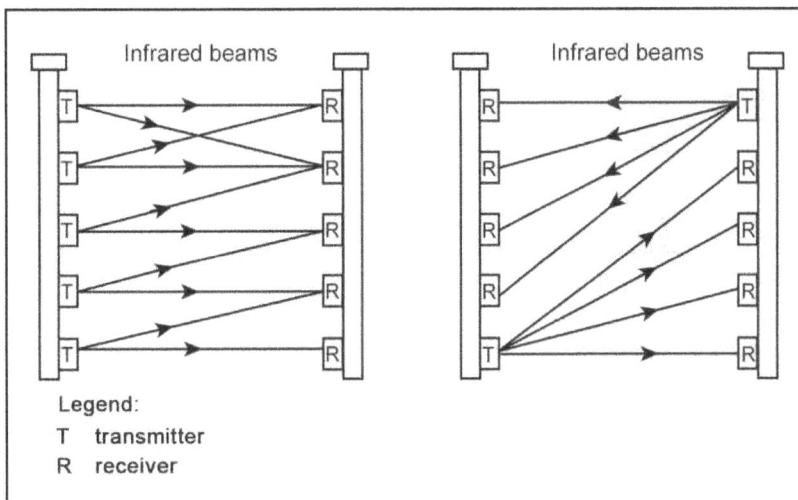

Figure 6-1. Common infrared-sensor beam patterns

Microwave Sensors

6-33. Microwave intrusion-detection sensors are categorized as bistatic or monostatic. Bistatic sensors use transmitting and receiving antennas located at opposite ends of the microwave link, whereas monostatic sensors use the same antenna.

- A bistatic system uses a transmitter and a receiver (separated by 100 to 1,200 feet) that are within direct line of sight of each other. The signal picked up by the receiver is the vector sum of the directly transmitted signal and signals that are reflected from the ground and nearby structures. Detection occurs when an object (intruder) moving within the beam pattern causes a change in net-vector summation of the received signals, resulting in variations of signal strength.

  - The same frequency bands allocated by the Federal Communications Commission for interior microwave sensors are also used for exterior sensors. Because high-frequency microwave beams are more directive than low-frequency beams, and the beam pattern is less affected by blowing grass in the area between the transmitter and the receiver, most exterior sensors operate at the next-to-highest allowable frequency—10.525 megahertz.

  - The shape of the microwave beam and the maximum separation between the transmitter and the receiver are functions of antenna size and configuration. Various antenna configurations are available, including parabolic-dish arrays, strip-line arrays, and slotted arrays. The parabolic antenna uses a microwave-feed assembly located at the focal point of a metallic parabolic reflector. A conical beam pattern is produced (see figure 6-2). A strip-line antenna configuration produces a nonsymmetrical beam that is higher than its height. Larger antenna configurations generally produce narrower beam patterns.

- Monostatic microwave sensors use the same antenna or virtually coincident antenna arrays for the transmitter and receiver, which are usually combined into a single package. Two types of monostatic sensors are available. Amplitude-modulated sensors detect changes in the net-vector summation of reflected signals similar to bistatic sensors. Frequency-modulated sensors operate on the Doppler principle—similar to interior microwave sensors. The detection pattern is typically shaped like a teardrop (see figure 6-3). Monostatic sensors can provide volumetric coverage of localized areas, such as in corners or around the base of critical equipment.

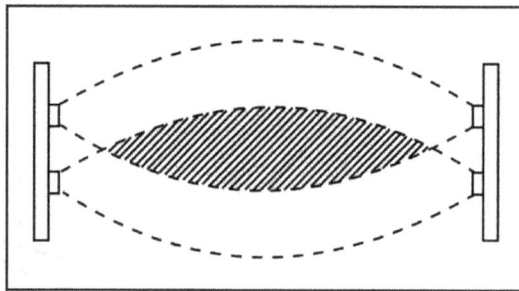

Figure 6-2. Typical nonsymmetrical beam pattern

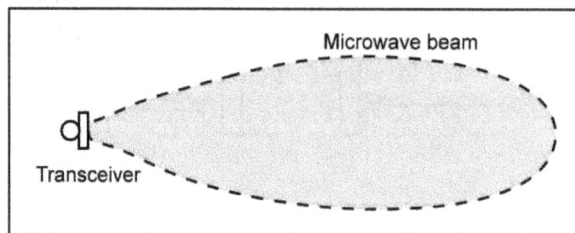

Figure 6-3. Typical monostatic-microwave-sensor detection pattern

Fiber-Optic Sensors

6-34. Fiber-optic cable sensors transmit modulated light down the cable, and the resulting received signals are processed to determine whether an alarm should be initiated. Since the cable contains no metal, and no electrical signal is present, fiber-optic sensors are generally less susceptible to electrical interference from lightning or other sources.

Buried Cable

6-35. A buried-line sensor system consists of detection probes or cable buried in the ground, typically between two fences that form an isolation zone. These devices are wired to an electronic processing unit. The processing unit generates an alarm if an intruder passes through the detection field. Buried-line sensors have several significant features:

- They are hidden, making them difficult to detect and circumvent.
- They follow the terrain's natural contour.
- They do not physically interfere with human activity, such as grass mowing or snow removal.
- They are affected by certain environmental conditions, such as running water and ground freeze/thaw cycles. (Seismic, seismic/magnetic, magnetic, and balanced pressure sensors are seldom used and are not discussed here.)

6-36. The ported coax cable sensor consists of two coax cables buried in the ground parallel to each other. An RF transmitter is connected to one cable and a receiver to the other. The outer conductor of each cable is ported (fabricated with small holes or gaps in the shield). The transmitter cable radiates RF energy into the medium surrounding the cables. A portion of this energy is coupled into the receiver cable through its ported shield. (Because of the ported shields, these cables are frequently referred to as leaky cables.) When an intruder enters the RF field, the coupling is disturbed, resulting in a change of signal monitored by the receiver, which then generates an alarm. Two basic types of ported coax sensors are available—pulse and continuous wave.

- A pulse-type sensor transmits a pulse of RF energy down one cable and monitors the received signal on the other. The cables can be up to 10,000 feet long. The signal processor initiates an alarm when the electromagnetic field created by the pulse is disturbed and identifies the disturbance's approximate location.
- Continuous-wave sensors apply continuous RF energy to one cable. The signal received on the other cable is monitored for electromagnetic-field disturbances that indicate an intruder's presence. Cable lengths are limited to 300 to 500 feet. The pattern typically extends 2 to 4 feet above the ground and can be 5 to 13 feet wide, depending on cable spacing and soil composition. Figure 6-4 represents a typical cross-section of a detection pattern created by a ported coax cable sensor.

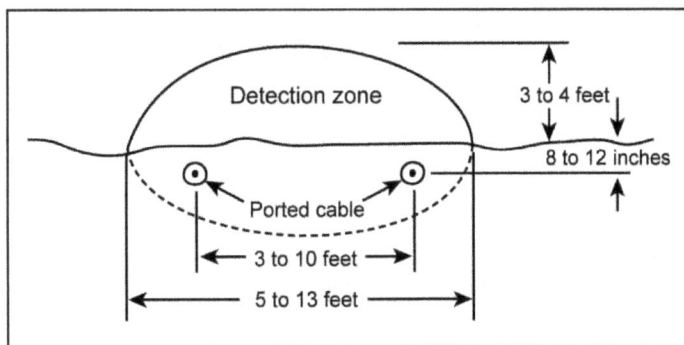

Figure 6-4. Typical ported coax cable detection pattern

INTERIOR SENSORS

6-37. Interior intrusion detection sensors are devices used to detect unauthorized entry into specific areas or volumetric spaces within a building. These sensors are usually not designed to be weatherproof—or are not rugged enough to survive an outdoor environment and should not be used outdoors, unless described by the manufacturer as suitable for outdoor use.

6-38. Interior intrusion detection sensors generally perform one of three detection functions—detection of an intruder penetrating the boundary of a protected area, detection of intruder motion within a protected area, or detection of an intruder touching or lifting an asset within a protected area. Therefore, interior sensors are commonly classified as point sensors and volumetric motion sensors.

Balanced Magnetic Switches

6-39. Balanced magnetic switches (BMSs) are interior-point sensors typically used to detect the opening of a door. These sensors can also be used on windows, hatches, gates, or other structural devices that can be opened to gain entry. When using a BMS, mount the switch mechanism on the doorframe and the actuating magnet on the door. Typically, the BMS has a three-position reed switch and an additional magnet (called the bias magnet) located adjacent to the switch. When the door is closed, the reed switch is held in the balanced or center position by interacting magnetic fields. If the door is opened, or an external magnet is brought near the sensor in an attempt to defeat it, the switch becomes unbalanced and generates an alarm. A BMS must be mounted so that the magnet receives maximum movement when the door or window is opened. Figure 6-5 shows several configurations for mounting a BMS.

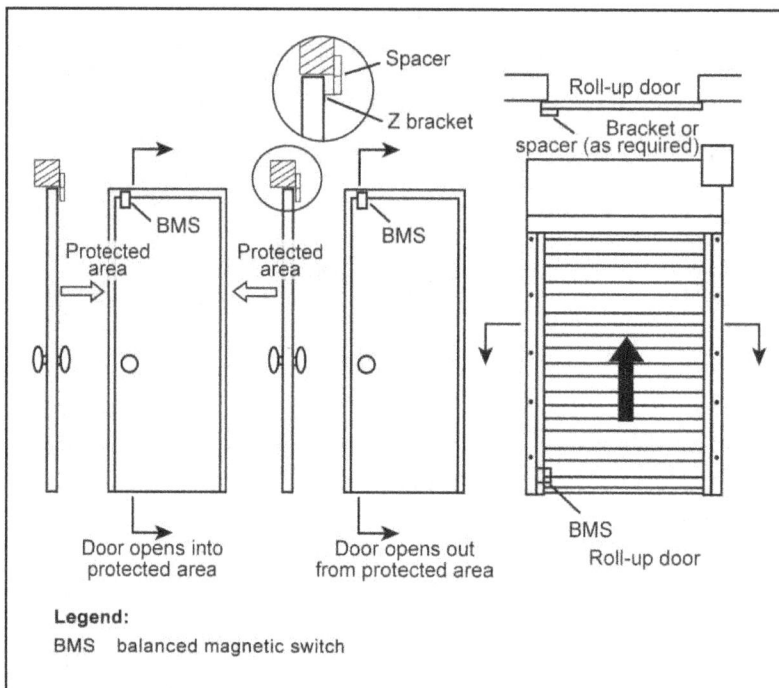

Figure 6-5. Balanced magnetic switches mounting configurations

Volumetric Motion Sensors

6-40. Volumetric motion sensors are designed to detect intruder motion within the interior of a protected volume. Volumetric sensors may be active or passive. Active sensors (such as microwave) fill the volume to be protected with an energy pattern and recognize a disturbance in the pattern when anything moves in the detection zone. Unlike active sensors that generate their own energy pattern to detect an intruder, passive sensors (such as IR) detect energy generated by an intruder. Some sensors, known as dual-technology sensors, use a combination of two different technologies, usually one active and one passive, within the same unit. If CCTV assessment or surveillance cameras are installed, video motion sensors can be employed to detect intruder movement in the area. Since ultrasonic motion sensors are seldom used, they will not be discussed in this manual.

Glass-Breakage Sensors

6-41. Glass-breakage sensors are volumetric motion sensors designed to detect the breaking of glass. The noise from breaking glass consists of frequencies in both the audible and ultrasonic range. Glass-breakage sensors use microphone transducers to detect the glass breakage. The sensors are designed to respond to specific frequencies and minimize false alarms caused by banging on the glass.

Passive Infrared Motion Sensors

6-42. The passive infrared (PIR) motion sensor is one of the most common interior volumetric intrusion-detection sensors. PIR motion sensors detect a change in the thermal energy pattern caused by a moving intruder and initiate an alarm when the change in energy satisfies the alarm criteria of the detector. These sensors are passive devices because they do not transmit energy; they monitor the energy radiated by the surrounding environment.

6-43. All objects with temperatures above absolute zero radiate thermal energy. The wavelengths of the IR energy spectrum lie between 1 and 1,000 microns. Because the human body radiates thermal energy of between 7 and 14 microns, PIR motion sensors are typically designed to operate in the far IR wavelength range of 4 to 20 microns.

6-44. The IR energy must be focused onto a sensing element, comparative to how a camera lens focuses light onto a film. Two techniques are common: One uses reflective focusing with parabolic mirrors to focus the energy, and the other uses an optical lens. Of the various types of optical lenses available, Fresnel lenses are preferred because they can achieve short focal lengths with minimal thickness. Because IR energy is severely attenuated by glass, lenses are usually made of plastic.

6-45. The detection pattern of the sensor is determined by the arrangement of lenses or reflectors. The pattern is not continuous but consists of a number of rays or fingers, one for each mirror or lens segment. Numerous detection patterns are available, several of which are shown in figure 6-6. The PIR is not provided with a range adjustment, but the range can be adjusted minimally by manipulating the position of the sensor; therefore, careful selection of the appropriate detection pattern is critical to proper sensor performance.

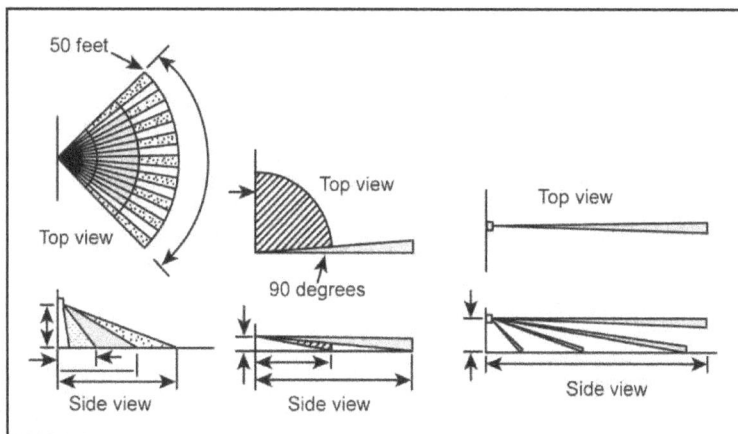

Figure 6-6. Typical detection patterns for a passive infrared motion detector

CLOSED-CIRCUIT TELEVISION SYSTEMS

6-46. The CCTV system is the integration of cameras, recorders, switches, keyboards, and monitors that allow viewing and recording of security events. The CCTV system is normally integrated into the overall ESS and centrally monitored at the security control center.

6-47. A properly integrated CCTV assessment system provides a rapid and cost-effective method for determining the cause of intrusion alarms. For surveillance, a properly designed CCTV system provides a cost-effective supplement to security operations. It is important to recognize that CCTV alarm-assessment systems and CCTV surveillance systems perform separate and distinct functions. The alarm-assessment system is designed to respond rapidly, automatically, and predictably to the receipt of ESS alarms at the security control center. The surveillance system is designed for use at the discretion and under the control of the console operator at the security control center. When the primary function of the CCTV system is to provide real-time alarm assessment, the design should incorporate a video-processing system that can communicate with the alarm-processing system.

6-48. A candidate site for a CCTV assessment system will typically have the following characteristics:
- Assets requiring ESS protection.
- A need for real-time alarm assessment.
- Protected assets spaced some distance apart.

6-49. Figure 6-7 shows a typical CCTV system configuration. A typical site will locate CCTV cameras—
- Outdoors, along site-perimeter isolation zones.
- Outdoors, at controlled access points (sally ports).
- Outdoors, in the protected area, and at viewing approaches to selected assets.
- Indoors, at selected assets in the protected area.

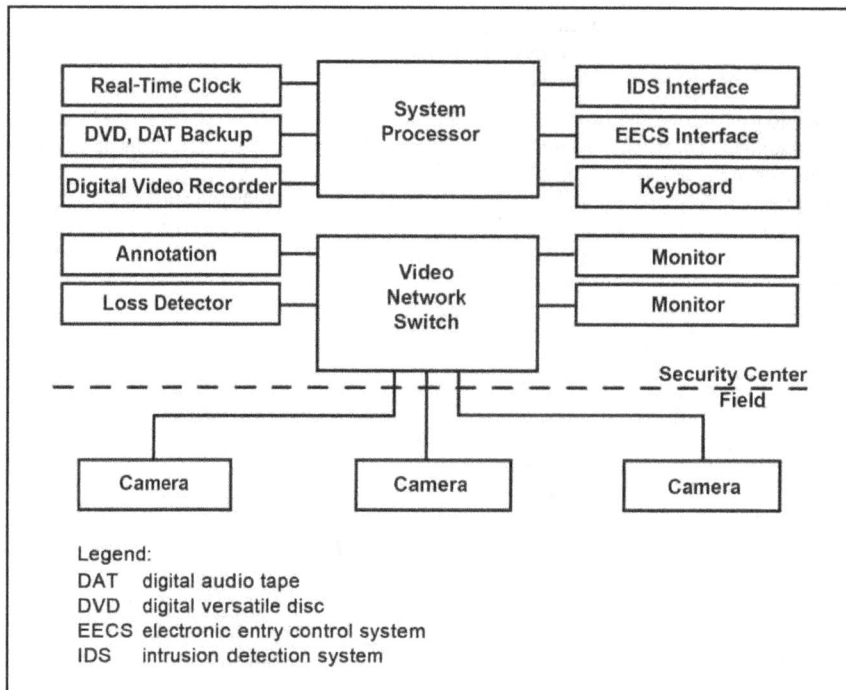

Figure 6-7. Closed-circuit television system configuration

6-50. The security console is centrally located in the security center. The CCTV monitors—and the ancillary video equipment—will be located at this console, as will the ESS alarm-processing and annunciation equipment.

CLOSED-CIRCUIT TELEVISION CAMERA COMPONENTS

6-51. An optical-lens system that captures and focuses reflected light from the scene being viewed onto an image target is common to all CCTV cameras. The image target converts reflected light energy into electrical impulses in a two-dimensional array of height and width. An electronic scanning system (reading these impulses in a predetermined order) creates a time-sensitive voltage signal that is a replica of optical information captured by the lens and focused on the target. This voltage signal is then transmitted to a location where it is viewed and possibly recorded. For components and technical information regarding CCTV cameras, see UFC 4-021-02NF and UFGS-28 23 23.00 10.

VIDEO SIGNAL AND CONTROL LINKS

6-52. A CCTV transmission system is needed to convey video signals from various facility cameras to the security center and to carry commands from the security center to the cameras. Information may be sent via the following methods:

- Metallic video cables are electrical conductors manufactured specifically for the transmission of frequencies associated with video components. Coaxial cable is a primary example of this type of transmission media. Devices such as video-equalization amplifiers, ground loop correctors, and video-distribution amplifiers may be required.
- RF transmission may be a good alternative to metallic cable and associated amplifiers for a system that has widely separated nodes. The information can be transmitted over a microwave link, which can be used for distances of about 50 miles, as long as the receiver and the transmitter are in the line of sight.
- In fiber-optic cable systems, electrical video signals are converted to optical light signals that are transmitted down the optical fiber. The signal is received and reconverted into electrical energy. An optic driver and a receiver are required per fiber. The fiber-optic transmission method provides a low-loss, high-resolution transmission system with usable length three to ten times that of traditional metallic cable systems. Fiber-optic cable is the transmission media favored by DA.

CLOSED-CIRCUIT TELEVISION SYSTEM SYNCHRONIZATION

6-53. Timing signals are processed within the image-scan section of the CCTV camera. These signals may be generated internally from a crystal clock, derived from the camera's alternating current (AC) power source or supplied by an external signal source. The camera should be capable of automatic switchover to its internal clock in case of external signal loss. When CCTV cameras are supplied by a common external (master) signal source or are all powered from the same AC power source, all cameras scan in synchronism. In this case, a console CCTV monitor will display a smooth transition when switched from one video source to another. Without this feature, the monitor display breaks up or rolls when switched between video sources. The rolling occurs for as long as it takes the monitor to synchronize its scan with that of the new video source—typically 1 second. The resynchronization delay will be experienced by all system components that receive video information, including recorders. To avoid this delay, the designer must specify that all cameras are powered from the AC power phase or must specify master synchronization for the design.

VIDEO PROCESSING AND DISPLAY COMPONENTS

6-54. The CCTV camera signals propagate through the video transmission system and through coverage at the security center. In very simple configurations with only a few cameras and monitors, a hardwired connection between each camera and console monitor is adequate. As the number of cameras increases, the need to manage and add supplemental information to camera signals also increases. Psychological testing has demonstrated that the efficiency of console-operator assessment improves as the number of console monitors is reduced, with the optimum number being four to six monitors.

6-55. The major components of the video-processor system are described below. They include the video switcher, the video-loss detector, the alarm-processor communication path, the master video-sync generator, digital video recorders (DVRs), and monitors.

- **Video switchers**. Video switchers are required when the number of cameras exceeds the number of console monitors or when a monitor must be capable of selecting video from one of many sources. Video switchers are capable of presenting any of multiple video images to various monitors, recorders, and so forth.

- **Video-loss detector**. Video-loss detectors sense the continued integrity of incoming camera signals.

- **Alarm-processor communication path**. There must be a means of rapid communication between the ESS alarm-annunciation and video-processor systems. The alarm processor must send commands that cause the video switcher to select the camera appropriate for the sensor reporting an alarm. The video-processor system must report system tampering or failures (such as loss of video) to the alarm processor. The path should also pass date-and-time synchronizing information between processors so that recorded video scenes and printed alarm logs are properly correlated.

- **Master video-sync generator**. The master video sync includes a crystal-controlled timing generator, distribution amplifiers, and a transmission link to each camera.

- **Digital video recorders**. DVRs provide the means to record alarm-event scenes in real time for later analysis. The DVR typically receives its input through dedicated video-switcher or matrix outputs. To support recorder playback, the recorder output is connected to a dedicated switcher input and must be compatible with the switcher-signal format. In addition, the DVR receives start commands from the switcher, and compatibility must exist at this interface. DVRs should be used when alarm events are to be recorded for later playback and analysis. Recorded events can be transferred to a digital versatile disc recorder or a compact disc recorder for purposes of capturing specific events during analysis—or archived, if required (see UFC 4-021-02NF).

- **Monitors**. Monitors are required to display the individual scenes transmitted from the cameras or from the video switcher. In alarm-assessment applications, the monitors are driven by dedicated outputs of the video switcher, and the monitors display video sources selected by the switcher. For security-console operations, the nine-inch monitor is the smallest screen that should be used for operator recognition of small objects in a camera's field of view. Two 9-inch monitors can be housed side by side in a standard 19-inch console. If the monitors are to be mounted in freestanding racks behind the security console, larger units will be used.

6-56. Video-processor equipment will be specified to append the following alphanumeric information so that it appears on both monitors and recordings. The equipment must allow the operator to program the annotated information and dictate its position on the screen. This information includes—

- Time and date information.
- Video-source or alarm-zone identification.
- Programmable titles.

CLOSED-CIRCUIT TELEVISION APPLICATION GUIDELINES

6-57. Site-specific factors must be considered in selecting components that comprise a CCTV system. Some factors include the size of the system in terms of the number of cameras fielded (which is the minimum number needed to view all ESS sensor-detection fields and surveillance camera); the requirement of some CCTV cameras for artificial light sources to work effectively; and CCTV system performance criteria and physical, environmental, and economic considerations. Each is discussed in detail in UFC 4-021-02NF.

Scene Resolution

6-58. The level to which video details can be determined in a CCTV scene is referred to as resolving ability or resolution. Three resolution requirements can be defined for assessment purposes. In order of increasing resolution requirements, they are detection, recognition, and identification.

- Detection is the ability to detect the presence of an object in a CCTV scene.
- Recognition is the ability to determine the type of object in a CCTV scene (such as an animal, blowing debris, or a crawling human).
- Identification is the ability to determine object details (such as a particular person, a large rabbit, or a small deer).

6-59. A CCTV assessment system should provide sufficient resolution to recognize human presence and to detect small animals or blowing debris. When an intrusion sensor alarms, it is critical that the console operator be able to determine if the sensor detected an intruder, or if it is responding to a nuisance condition (refer to UFC 4-021-02NF).

Illumination Levels

6-60. For interior applications where the same camera type is used in several different areas and the scene illumination in each area is constant, the manually adjustable iris must be specified. This allows a manual iris adjustment appropriate for the illumination level of each area at the time of installation. If the camera must operate in an area subject to a wide dynamic range of illumination levels (such as outdoors), the automatically adjusted iris feature must be specified. TM 5-811-1 provides further information on designing lighting systems for use with CCTV.

Cost Considerations

6-61. The cost of a CCTV system is usually quoted as cost-per-assessment zone. When estimating the total system cost, video-processor equipment costs and the video-transmission costs of the system must be included. Other potentially significant costs are outdoor lighting system upgrades and the site preparation required to support the CCTV cameras. The CCTV systems are expensive, compared to other electronic security subsystems, and should be specified with discretion.

DATA-TRANSMISSION MEDIA

6-62. A critical element in an integrated ESS design is the DTM that transmits information from sensors, entry-control devices, and video components to displays and assessment equipment. A DTM link is a path for transmitting data between two or more components (such as a sensor and alarm reporting system, a card reader and controller, a CCTV camera and monitor, or a transmitter and receiver). The DTM links connect remote ESS components to the security center and notify the response force of an intrusion.

6-63. A number of different media are used in transmitting data for electronic security data transmission. These include hardwired, cellular, encrypted Internet data transmission, voice-over Internet protocol, direct subscriber lines, wireless, and free-space optics.

HARDWIRED

6-64. Hardwired DTM uses dedicated proprietary (DOD-owned) conductors to transmit data/video between DTM nodes. Hardwired DTM is very good for security when totally contained on DOD property. The dedicated conductors can be copper or fiber optics.

- **Copper conductors**. Copper conductors can be run 750 to 1500 feet, depending on the type of connectors used. Longer distances are possible using repeaters. Copper conductors are susceptible to electromagnetic interference, radio-frequency interference, and damage from lighting strikes.
- **Fiber optics**. Fiber-optic cables use the wide bandwidth properties of light traveling through transparent fibers. Fiber optics is a reliable communication medium best suited for point-to-point, high-speed data transmission. It is immune to RF electromagnetic interference and does not produce electromagnetic radiation emission. The preferred DTM for an ESS is fiber-optic cables, unless there are justifiable economic or technical reasons for using other types of media.

DIRECT SUBSCRIBER LINES

6-65. Direct subscriber lines, also called T-1 lines, are commonly used in data transmission media systems for connecting remote sites. T-1 lines are permanent point-to-point links through public networks. These lines are uniquely assigned so that only the DOD information is to be transmitted over the assigned conductors (typically fiber optics). For security, T-1 lines are the second- or third-best option.

WIRELESS

6-66. For security reasons, only use wireless if other media cannot be used. Wireless broadband networks make use of RF transmission between towers. Wireless communications are affected by line-of-sight topography and extreme weather conditions. Security can be achieved by vendor encryption and decryption at each node. Wireless systems are susceptible to jamming. From a security standpoint, this option may be adequate on DOD property if there is little chance of interception.

FREE-SPACE OPTICS

6-67. Free-space optics refers to the transmission of modulated visible or IR beams through the atmosphere to obtain broadband communications. Its operation is similar to fiber-optics transmission, except that information is transmitted through space rather than a fiber-optic cable. Free-space optics can function over distances of several kilometers, but does require clear line of sight unless mirrors are used to reflect the light energy. Advantages include reduced construction cost (no lines have to be installed). Limitations include the ability of rain, snow, dust, fog, or smog to block the transmission path and shut down the network.

6-68. Data links used to communicate the status of ESS devices or other sensitive information to the security center must be protected from possible compromise. Attempts to defeat the security system may range from simple efforts to cut or short the transmission line to more sophisticated undertakings, such as tapping and substituting bogus signals. Data links can be made more secure by physical protection, tamper protection, line supervision, and encryption.

SECURITY CONTROL CENTER

6-69. The Security Control Center, sometimes referred to as the Dispatch Center or Site Security Control Center (see AR 190-59), serves as a central monitoring and assessment space for the access control and CCTV and IDS. It is the control point for all security operations for the installation and the monitoring point for protective alarm and communication systems. The Security Control Center is the critical control point for security situational awareness for the installation. The center includes assessment; monitoring; integration of dispatch communications; and receiving alerts from IDS alarms, access control sensors, and CCTV sensors.

6-70. Normally, the Security Control Center is under the command and control of the designated provost marshal or director of emergency services. The center is staffed by trained personnel and operates 24 hours a day, 7 days a week. The Security Control Center may be centrally located on the installation or collocated with other installation functions. A separate security office may be necessary at the installation's ACP to coordinate and monitor access control activities.

6-71. Security facilities are often a priority target for adversaries. As such, security facilities should be designed with adequate protection and standoff distances that protect personnel, operations, and equipment.

Chapter 7

Access Control Points

The *access control point* is a corridor at the installation entrance through which all vehicles and pedestrians must pass when entering or exiting the installation. The objective of an ACP is to secure the installation from unauthorized access and intercept contraband such as weapons, explosives, illegal drugs, and classified material while maximizing vehicular traffic flow. This chapter does not make a distinction between entry control points and ACPs. For conciseness, the term ACP is used throughout this publication to describe the overall layout, organization, infrastructure, facilities, and activities of the ACP.

The perimeter of the ACP consists of both passive and active barriers, arranged to form a contiguous barrier to pedestrians and vehicles. Soldiers, civilian guards, or automated equipment control the barriers to deny or permit entry into the area. The design of an ACP should ensure that vehicles are contained through an arrangement of passive and active vehicle barrier systems. The primary objective of the design is to prevent an unauthorized vehicle or pedestrian from entering the installation. The standard design does not provide a one-size-fits-all solution. Each installation is unique and will require an engineered solution with input from planners, designers, and security personnel. The factors of mission, enemy, terrain and weather, troops and support available, time available, and civil considerations (METT-TC) determines the level of self-protection needed at an ACP. Protection measures should be appropriate for the anticipated level of threat. Armored vehicles, security overwatch, and fighting positions are used when necessary.

POLICY AND TECHNICAL GUIDANCE

7-1.   AR 190-13 prescribes physical security policies and procedures for Army installation access control. The Army Access Control Points Standard Definitive Design and Criteria manual controls Army ACP design by incorporating requirements from Office of the Provost Marshal General and standards from the Assistant Chief of Staff for Installation Management and the United States Army Corps of Engineers (USACE). It also provides design procedures for incorporating safety into ACP designs, especially with respect to barrier placement.

7-2.   Technical criteria for the standards, planning, design, and support guidance for DOD entry/ACPs can be found in UFC 4-010-01, UFC 4-020-01, and UFC 4-022-01.

7-3.   In addition to the UFC manuals mentioned above, there is a series of additional UFC manuals that provides detailed design guidance for developing final designs. These support manuals provide specialized, discipline-specific design guidance. Some address specific tactics, such as direct fire weapons, forced entry, or airborne contamination. Others address details of designs for specific protective measures, such as vehicle barriers or fences.

ACCESS CONTROL POINT SITE SELECTION

7-4.   Site selection for a new ACP starts with an extensive evaluation of the anticipated demand for access to the installation, an analysis of traffic origin and destination, and an analysis of the capability of the surrounding road network to tie in to the ACP, including its capacity to handle additional traffic. Analyses of traffic patterns at installation entry points should include the local Department of Transportation since any traffic changes will likely have some effect or impact on civilian traffic patterns (see UFC 4-022-01).

7-5.   If the site is expected to have a high-traffic volume, a traffic control study is normally conducted to determine ACP requirements. Military police and engineers are specially trained to collect and analyze data to determine traffic volume and patterns. The results of the study will ensure the proper placement of an ACP with consideration to the surrounding community. A well-designed ACP will maximize the flow of traffic without compromising safety and security or causing undue delays that may affect the mission of the installation or off-post public highway use.

ACCESS CONTROL POINT CLASSIFICATIONS, FUNCTIONS, AND ZONES

7-6.   An ACP is classified based on the intended function and its anticipated use—referred to as the four "use" classifications (see UFC 4-022-01). The use classification is a function of the type of traffic, hours of operation, and FPCON considerations. Table 7-1 highlights the ACP use classifications.

Table 7-1. Access control point classifications

Use Classification	Operational Hours	FPCON Considerations	Preferred Operation
Primary	24/7 Open continuously	Open thru FPCON Delta	Vehicle registration/visitor pass capacity. Regular operations, visitors with authorization. Could also be designated as truck and delivery gate.
Secondary	Regular hours, closed at times	Potentially closed at or above FPCON Charlie	Regular operations, visitors with authorization. Could also be designated as truck and delivery gate.
Limited Use	Only opened for special purposes	Closed at most times	Tactical vehicles, HAZMAT, special events, etc.
Pedestrian Access	Varies	Potentially closed at or above FPCON Charlie	Personnel only. Could be located near installation housing areas, near schools, or as part of a Primary or Secondary ACP.
Legend: ACP access control point FPCON force protection condition HAZMAT hazardous material			

ACCESS CONTROL POINT FUNCTION CLASSIFICATION

7-7.   While the primary mission of the ACP is access control, there are many functions that take place there. Not all functions are required at every ACP, but are instead based on the installation's mission, antiterrorism plan, ACP classification, and land area. At higher FPCON levels, functions may change; however, basic functions associated with an ACP include—

- Processing visitors.
- Vehicle identification checks.
- Personnel identification checks.
- Vehicle inspections.
- Commercial/large vehicle inspections.

7-8. Functional requirements may be combined when there are a limited number of access points. Speed and efficiency are improved when passenger cars and trucks are instructed to use separate lanes and separate search facilities.

ACCESS CONTROL POINT ZONES

7-9. An ACP begins with a corridor that is divided into four zones, each encompassing specific functions and operations. Beginning at the installation boundary is the corridor through which all vehicles and pedestrians must pass when entering and exiting. Once vehicles and pedestrians have passed into the corridor, they approach and enter each zone as permitted by access control Soldiers/guards and devices (see UFC 4-022-01).

APPROACH ZONE

7-10. The approach zone runs between the ACP entrance to the beginning of the access control zone. It is the area that all vehicles must pass through before reaching the actual checkpoint. Specific functions that occur in the approach zone are—

● Reducing the speed of incoming vehicles.

● Sorting and queuing vehicles for identification authentication.

● Providing adequate queuing distance for vehicles waiting for entry to ensure minimal impact on traffic flow offsite.

● Providing an appropriate standoff distance for responding to threat vehicles with the appropriate level of force.

7-11. The approach zone should be designed to accommodate peak traffic times without impeding the offpost traffic flow. Maximize the length of the approach zone to provide optimal stacking distance for the traffic queue. Reversible lanes can increase throughput and flexibility where space is unavailable for additional lanes. However, reversible lanes should only be used if all other design options have been considered. Reversible lanes must be properly designed according to UFC and Army standards.

7-12. The approach zone should have the capability to sort vehicles by type. Normally, trucks use the farthest right lane. Separating vehicles with varying inspection requirements can also increase traffic flow. Consider authorized personnel using a separate lane with automated access control.

7-13. Speed management should be used for inbound lanes to slow vehicles before they reach the access control zone. Slowing vehicles in the approach zone allows security personnel adequate time to respond to unauthorized activities. The preferred method for speed management is to use road alignment, such as serpentine. While road alignment is the best method for slowing traffic in the approach zone if trucks are considered, the ability to control passenger vehicle speed is affected. Large cargo vehicle traffic should be separated for optimum serpentine use. Figure 7-1, page 7-4, illustrates a typical serpentine road alignment (road width 20 feet) designed to slow vehicles in the approach zone.

7-14. Table 7-2, page 7-4, provides separation distance for barriers to reduce speed for passenger cars.

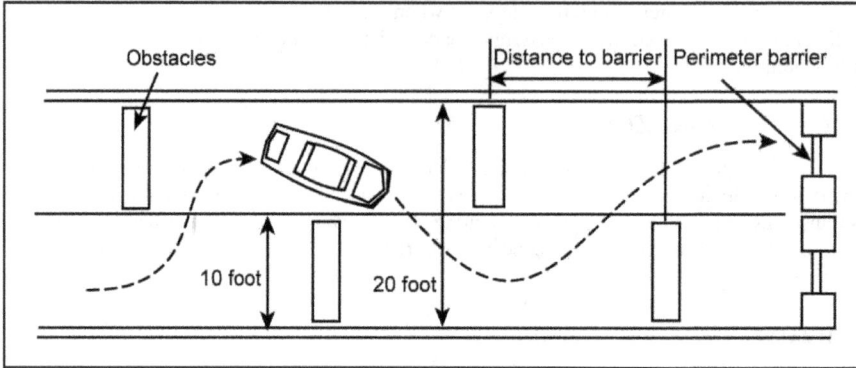

Figure 7-1. Serpentine pattern road alignment

Table 7-2. Separation distance for barriers to reduce speed on straight path

Achievable Speed of Vehicle in mph (kph) →	20 mph (32)	30 mph (48)	40 mph (64)	50 mph (80)
Road Width in ft (m) ↓	Barrier Distances	Barrier Distances	Barrier Distances	Barrier Distances
20 ft (6.1)	28 ft (8.5)	43 ft (13.1)	58 ft (17.7)	73 ft (22.2)
30 ft (9.1)	40 ft (12.2)	63 ft (19.2)	86 ft (26.2)	108 ft (32.9)
40 ft (12.2)	47 ft (14.3)	77 ft (23.5)	106 ft (32.3)	134 ft (40.8)
50 ft (15.2)	51 ft (15.5)	87 ft (26.5)	122 ft (37.2)	155 ft (47.2)
Legend:				
ft feet				
kph kilometers per hour				
m meters				
mph miles per hour				

ACCESS CONTROL ZONE

7-15. The access control zone is the primary controlling element of the ACP and lies between the approach and response zones. This zone includes the gatehouse and the traffic management equipment used in support of the duties of the access controllers. The purpose of the access control zone is to determine the authorization of a vehicle to enter. Typically, the identity of every occupant in a vehicle is verified via picture identification. Access verification may be conducted by Soldiers/guards or automated means and may result in a vehicle being given authorized access or being directed to another area of the ACP. Inspections conducted in the access control zone are conducted according to Training Circular (TC) 19-210, applicable ARs, and locally established security procedures.

7-16. The access control zone should be designed to manage authorized vehicles and personnel, reject unauthorized vehicles, and minimize the adverse impacts on traffic flow. Since this is the area where access control personnel most often perform their tasks, this zone should provide cover with an overhead canopy to protect against inclement weather, facilitate identification and inspection procedures, and provide a platform for lighting, detection, and surveillance equipment.

7-17. Rejection points should be located before the central identification area, and another should occur just beyond the identification area. If only one rejection point is possible, it should be located beyond the identification area.

RESPONSE ZONE

7-18. The response zone is the area extending from the end of the access control zone to the final active vehicle barrier. This zone defines the end of the ACP. The purpose of the response zone is to allow the security force to respond to a threat, operate the active vehicle barriers, and close the ACP, if necessary. Commanders should consider lethal and nonlethal response capabilities. Nonlethal capabilities provide an alternative to lethal force in environments where lethal force is not the preferred option.

7-19. The response zone should be designed with sufficient length to provide adequate reaction time for the security force to respond to a threat. Place final denial barriers at the end of the response zone to stop threat vehicles from using high-speed attacks to gain forced entry to the installation. The length of the response zone and placement of the final barriers are based on providing adequate response time. Refer to the Army Access Control Points Standard Definitive Design and Criteria for determining length of response zone and estimating response time. Depending on the design and area available for the ACP, positive speed control measures—such as roadway geometry or obstacles—may be necessary in the response zone to allow adequate time for barrier deployment.

SAFETY ZONE

7-20. The safety zone extends from the active and passive vehicle barriers that define the boundary of the ACP. Establishing an appropriate safety zone reduces the effects of a potential explosion near the ACP. Consider the effects an explosion may have on nearby personnel, buildings, or assets. Determine the acceptable standoff distance or safety zone by the expected weight of the explosive charge and the facility or asset to be protected. Refer to UFC 4-010-02 to determine proper standoff distances.

7-21. Based on the assumed explosive weight, injury levels can be predicted based on distance from the explosion. The user must make decisions based on the risk involved and the probability that an incident would take place. Consider high-value assets such as mission-critical, high-profile facilities or structures close to the ACP with a high concentration of personnel as high risk.

INSPECTION PROCEDURES

7-22. Army installations and facilities focus first on threats that can be mitigated at the first line of defense—the installation perimeter. The ACP is a part of the installation perimeter and a legal line of demarcation. Installation commanders should establish appropriate rules governing the entry and exit of installations. This includes the inherent responsibility to conduct inspections of personnel and vehicles. The purpose of an inspection is to determine and ensure the security, military fitness, and good order and discipline on the installation.

7-23. Inspections at ACPs are not based on probable cause to believe that the vehicle/pedestrian is carrying contraband or weapons but on the commander's authority to protect the security of the installation, protect government property, and to protect personnel. All personnel entering an Army installation are subject to inspections. Individuals who object to an inspection upon entry may be denied access. All personnel are subject to inspections upon leaving an installation regardless of their objections.

7-24. The installation commander issues specific written instructions that state the times, location, scope, and method of the inspections. Inspection procedures should accommodate RAMs for sustained operations and should be designed, manned, and equipped to operate at all FPCON, including 100-percent vehicle inspections.

VEHICLE INSPECTIONS

7-25. Security personnel should be familiar with the inspection procedures described in TC 19-210, which discuss the legal and jurisdictional issues associated with vehicle inspections and provide the basic elements necessary for effective access control operations.

7-26. The Vehicle Inspection Guide Training Support Package developed by the Technical Support Working Group is a training tool available to federal, state, and local governments involved in security and antiterrorism activities. The Vehicle Inspection Guide Training Support Package supports the field use of the Vehicle Inspection Guide publication, available through the Government Printing Office, e-mail pubs@ tswg.gov, GPO stock number 008-001-00184-3.

7-27. Specific procedures for vehicle inspections should be established for each installation. Procedures are based on the threat assessment, mission of the installation, available manpower, and availability of specialized security equipment—such as vapor sensors, cargo X-ray, and explosive detection devices. General guidelines for conducting vehicle inspections include the following:

- Security personnel direct driver to vehicle inspection area.
- Driver is instructed to dismount and open all compartments, doors, hood, and trunk.
- Driver and passenger remain with the vehicle or move to a holding area close by. Driver and passenger remain under constant observation by security personnel not involved in the inspection of the vehicle.
- Inspection team conducts a systematic search of the vehicle that includes—
  - Vehicle exterior.
  - Engine compartment.
  - Vehicle trunk.
  - Vehicle interior.
- The external portion of the vehicle—
  - Inspect from the bottom of the vehicle and work to the top.
  - Look for body repairs, freshly painted sections, anything indicating altering or tampering with the external surface of the vehicle.
  - Use an appropriate light source and creeper to carefully inspect under the vehicle. Mirrors are useful but generally provide limited view of the undercarriage.
  - Check the suspension, drive train, wheel wells, bumpers, under the engine, and above the gas tank.
  - Look for any unusual devices, weld marks, new bolts/screws, alterations, and signs of tampering to the undercarriage.
- Inside the engine compartment—
  - Pause and observe everything in view; then start at the outer edge where the battery is located, and work toward the center of the engine.
  - Look for additional wires running from the battery.
  - Look for out-of-place or unusually clean components, devices, and wiring and electrical tape.
  - Check under large components such as the air breather, fan blade, and fluid reservoirs.
  - Look for signs of alteration or tampering with any components in the engine compartment.
- Inside the truck compartment—
  - Pause and observe everything in view; then begin at the edge and inspect inward.
  - Pay close attention to packages. Have the driver open bags, packages, boxes, and containers.
  - Look for signs of electrical tape, wire, stripped wire insulation, string, fine wire, fishing line, or unusual electrical components.
  - Look for hidden compartments.
  - Inspect the tire well, tire jack, and tool storage areas.
  - Look for additional wires attached to the brake lights or rear turn signals.
  - Look closely at the area behind the rear seat for signs of alteration or tampering.
- Inside the driver and passenger compartment—
  - Pause and observe everything in view; then start at the floor and work up. Look for anything unusual or out of place. Have the driver open any packages, bags, or containers.
  - Look for bits of wire, electrical tape, stripped insulation, or unusual electrical components on the floor, dash, or seats.
  - Check under the dash, floor mats, seats, and in the glove compartment.
  - Check the door panels for signs of tampering.

- Check the roof lining for signs of possible concealment of explosives.
- Look for signs of alteration and tampering, paying close attention to any new or exposed wiring.

7-28. Inspections of cargo vehicles may require special cargo X-ray systems such as the Nonintrusive Inspection System. This system is designed to provide thorough image processing for complex or dense cargo. The Nonintrusive Inspection System requires a Field System Representative, who provides the technical expertise. Users are required to provide adequate ground power and must be in a Radiation Safety Program.

MILITARY WORKING DOG SUPPORT

7-29. The specialized ability for MWDs to detect explosives makes them a valuable asset for vehicle inspection activities. Bomb dogs are trained with a passive response to scents and compounds used in bomb making. They provide a more thorough detection capability for security personnel and add an element of deterrence for potential adversaries.

7-30. When using MWDs for vehicle inspections, instruct the driver and occupants to move to a holding area while the dog conducts the search. In the event the dog indicates the presence of explosives, the MWD team and security personnel withdraw immediately from the vehicle. The driver and occupant are detained, the area is evacuated, and explosive ordnance disposal personnel are notified. The MWD team remains in the area at a safe distance in case the explosive ordnance disposal team requests further detector assistance (see FM 3-19.17).

IDENTIFICATION DOCUMENTS

7-31. Homeland Security Presidential Directive-12 (HSPD-12) mandates policy for a common identification standard for all Federal employees and contractors. The FIPS 201-2 provides standards for the identity verification, issuance, and use of the common identity standard. The DOD Federal personal identity verification credential, known as the common access card (CAC), is the principal individual identity credential for supporting access to installations, facilities, buildings, and controlled spaces. The CAC, when properly presented at perimeter security locations, is accepted for perimeter security screening purposes.

7-32. Occasional visitors to military installations and facilities use a locally established, temporary-issue, visitor identification system. Typically, government photo identification (such as a valid state driver's license) is required to gain access to any Army installation or facility. However, non-DOD visitors and children under a certain age may not have government-issued identification. Procedures for authorized access for such visitors should be developed and included in the security instructions at each ACP.

7-33. ACPs should be designed to have an identity check area where security personnel or automated equipment verify pedestrians, vehicles, and occupants identification. Security personnel physically take the identification card and compare the picture on the card to the owner (see TC 19-210). Other measures to verify the card include checking the following:

- Expiration date.
- Both sides of the card.
- Physical characteristics against the person's physical appearance.
- Signs that the card has been altered.

EXAMINING HAND-CARRIED ITEMS

7-34. Security personnel are often required to check hand-carried items—which is an examination, not a search. During the examination, have the person open the item and reveal the contents. If an item is discovered at this time that may cause a safety concern, stop the check and notify the security officer. If a person refuses an examination of his or her hand-carried item, deny that person entry, follow local procedures, and notify the security officer.

7-35. Security personnel should look for firearms, knives, and explosive materials. If a person is discovered in possession of a firearm or explosives, maintain control of the firearm or device, detain the person, and notify the security officer. If the item appears to pose an immediate threat, do not handle the item, clear the area to a safe distance, detain the person and secure the area, and notify the supporting explosive ordnance disposal personnel.

7-36. Security personnel should have specific written instructions on procedures to follow when encountering explosives and other dangerous items.

Chapter 8

Key Control and Locking Systems Security

A lock is the most accepted and widely used security device; however, it is only a delay device and should never be considered as a stand-alone method of security. Some locks require considerable time and expert manipulation to open, but all locks can be defeated by force or with the proper tools. The best defense for locking devices is an effective key-control program. A key policy is intended to govern the control of keys and locks. Its purpose is to maintain access to facilities, while better safeguarding the personal safety of the people who live and work on the facility; to protect critical assets; and to avoid potentially significant costs due to theft, damage, or criminal activity. The systematic control of keys and locks is one of the most important components of any security program. Without proper key control, locks provide little deterrence to unauthorized entry into a facility.

KEY AND LOCK CUSTODIAN AND ALTERNATE CUSTODIAN

8-1. Regardless of whether a custodian is supporting an administrative or AA&E key control program, both the primary and alternate key and lock custodians are appointed in writing to issue, receive and maintain accountability for keys and locking systems and, where applicable, lock combinations. An administrative key and lock custodian is accountable for office, unit, or activity keys and locking systems and—

- Ensures that individuals designated to issue, receive, and account for keys in his or her absence understand local key control procedures.
- Maintains a key control register at all times to ensure continuous accountability for keys of locks used to secure government property.
- Ensures that he or she is listed on unit and facility access rosters where appropriate.
- Carries out the duties required for key and lock accountability.

KEY AND LOCK CONTROLS FOR ADMINISTRATIVE ACCOUNTABILITY

8-2. Key and lock controls, key containers, and depositories for AA&E and administrative key control are separate systems, covered by different regulations. AA&E key control is described in AR 190-11, paragraph 3-8. Administrative key control is described in AR 190-51, appendix D.

8-3. Primary and alternate key and lock custodians are responsible for key and lock accountability and reconciling discrepancies on the key roster. Only the commander and the key custodian (or alternate) issue and receive keys to and from individuals on the key access roster.

8-4. Key and lock custodians maintain a record to identify each key, lock, and lock combination used by the activity, including replacement or reserve keys and locks. When not in use, the key control register is kept in a locked container that does not contain or store classified material and to which access is controlled (AR 190-51). The record should show—

- Current building or entrances that the key or lock secures.
- Number and identification (serial number) of keys issued.
- Who has custody of each key or lock.
- Location and number of duplicate keys for each lock.
- Lock serial numbers.
- Number and location of locks and keys held in reserve.

8-5.   The commander should consider a policy for the key and lock custodian's duties, which may include procurement and receipt of keys and locks and investigation of lost or stolen keys. When a key to a lock is lost or missing, an inquiry is conducted immediately. Locks and lock cores are changed when keys are lost or stolen. All keys and duplicate keys that are not in use are stored in a key depository.

8-6.   No key holder is authorized to duplicate any keys. Commanders may consider marking all keys with the phrase "DO NOT DUPLICATE." When duplicate keys are required, the process should be according to AR 190-51. Master keys are not to be used except as outlined in AR 190-51. Padlocks and keys that do not have a serial number are given one. This number is inscribed on the lock or key as appropriate.

8-7.   Replacement of lock cylinders and broken keys for high-security locks may be requested through normal supply channels. Requests are coordinated through the key control custodian. Army Service Component Commands are designated as approval authorities for a deviation in key procurement procedures.

8-8.   Combinations to all combination locks, such as padlocks, coded door locks, safes, and vault/armory doors, are changed according to AR 380-5. Combinations will be changed—

- When locks are first placed in use.
- Whenever an individual knowing the combination no longer requires access.
- When the combination has been subject to possible compromise.
- At least once annually.
- When taken out of service, built–in combination locks will be reset to the standard combination 50–25–50; combination padlocks will be reset to the standard combination 10–20–30.
- Annually, per United States Central Registry, when North Atlantic Treaty Organization information is stored in the security container, vault, or secure room.

8-9.   When a chain is required for security of unclassified, nonsensitive equipment and supplies, the custodian can obtain chain specifications from the Naval Facilities Engineering Service Center, ATTN: DOD Lock Program, 1100 23d Avenue, Port Hueneme, California 93043-4370 (800) 290-7607, commercial (805) 982-1212, Defense Switched Network (DSN): 551-1212.

8-10.   Additional key and lock controls for IDS and IDS key containers and for aircraft and vehicle storage are addressed in AR 190-51.

KEY AND LOCK CONTROLS FOR ARMS, AMMUNITION, AND EXPLOSIVES AND KEY CONTAINERS/DEPOSITORIES

8-11.   A lockable container, such as a safe or filing cabinet, or a key depository made of at least 20-gauge steel for AA&E and 26-gauge steel for unclassified property, equipped with a tumbler-type locking device and permanently affixed to a wall, is used to secure keys. The key depository is located in a room with 24-hour surveillance or in a locked room when unoccupied. AR 190-11 prescribes policy and procedures for AA&E key control requirements.

8-12.   An automated lockable key container is authorized, provided the container meets United States General Services Administration (GSA) standards and generates a record of key use. Ensure that the electronic key container is properly programmed, permitting only authorized personnel access to duty-specific keys. The printer record must contain the name of the individual receiving the key, date and time of issuance, and date and time returned. A printed record will be produced each time a key is removed and returned. In case of a system failure, detailed instructions must be included in the lock and key SOP on how accountability is maintained, along with information on emergency access to the keys stored in the automated container (see AR 190-11).

8-13.   Keys to AA&E storage buildings, rooms, racks, containers, and IDS may be secured together in the same key container, but are stored separately from other keys (such as administrative keys). Under no circumstances are keys and locks or alternate keys or locks placed in a security container that contains or stores classified material. The keys to AA&E storage buildings, rooms, racks, containers, and IDS are accessible only to those individuals whose official duties require access to them and whose names and information appear on the key control access roster (described in paragraph 8-14). Keys to these areas and items are never removed from the installation except to provide for protected storage elsewhere. The keys to locks securing key containers are afforded physical protection equivalent to that provided by the key container itself. A duplicate set of keys to AA&E should be maintained at higher headquarters.

8-14. A current roster of individuals who are allowed access to these keys is maintained in the unit, agency, or organization. The roster is signed by a designated official and is protected from public view. A key is not issued to a person not listed on the roster. A key control register is maintained at the unit level to ensure continuous accountability for keys, ensure positive control of keys, and establish responsibility for the custody of stored sensitive government equipment and AA&E. Use and maintenance of the key register is described below.

8-15. A semiannual inventory of keys and locks by serial number is conducted. The inventory is recorded and maintained in unit files for a minimum of 1 year. Padlocks and keys without a number are inscribed with a number different from the numbers on other padlocks and keys.

8-16. Keys required for maintenance and repair of IDS, including keys to the control unit door and monitor cabinet, are maintained separately from other IDS keys. Access to the keys is permitted only to authorized IDS maintenance personnel.

8-17. IDS operational keys are stored in containers of at least 20-gauge steel equipped with GSA-approved, low-security padlocks; GSA-approved, built-in, three-position changeable combination locks; or in GSA-approved Class 5 or Class 6 containers that do not contain or store classified material. Combinations are recorded on Standard Form (SF) 700, Security Container Information, sealed in the envelope provided, and stored in a container per AR 380-5.

8-18. Containers holding AA&E keys weighing less than 500 pounds are fastened to the structure with bolts or chains equipped with secondary padlocks to preclude easy removal.

KEY REGISTER USE

8-19. The key and lock custodian maintains a key control register at all times to ensure continuous accountability for keys of locks used to secure unit facilities and AA&E. DA Form 5513 (Key Control Register and Inventory) is approved for use to meet the requirements of a key control register. Appendix E illustrates a properly filled out DA Form 5513.

8-20. Keys are issued to authorize personnel (determined from the unit access roster) on the key control register. Key control registers contain the printed name and signature of the individual receiving the key, date and hour of issuance, serial number or other identifying information of the key, printed name and signature of the person issuing the key, the date and hour that key was returned, and the printed name and signature of the individual receiving the returned key. Completed key control registers are retained in files for a minimum of 90 days for administrative registers and for 1 year for AA&E registers, and then they are disposed of per established Army command procedures.

8-21. When not in use, the key control register is kept in a locked container that does not contain or store classified material and to which access is controlled. Keys to locks securing key containers are afforded physical protection equivalent to that provided by the key container itself.

8-22. Keys for locks in use that protect the property of an office, unit, or activity are checked at the end of each duty day. Differences between keys on hand and the key control register are reconciled. Keys for locks associated with AA&E are turned in immediately upon completion of their need.

TYPES OF LOCKING DEVICES

8-23. The degree of protection afforded by a vault, a safe, or a filing cabinet may be measured in terms of the resistance of a lock. AR 50-5, AR 50-6, AR 190-11, AR 190-17, AR 190-51, AR 190-54, and AR 190-59 prescribe specific types of locks for specific types of facilities. AR 380-5 prescribes standard facilities for storing classified material and provides guidance for different storage requirements. The DOD Lock Program provides management, operation, and support functions for development, testing, and procurement of locking devices, security containers, and related delay devices. Appendix B provides the Technical Support Hotline information and link to their website.

8-24. Padlocks and keys not in use are secured in a locked container that does not contain or store classified material. Access to the container must be controlled. Locks should be opened and closed to verify that they are in working order and that the locks can be opened and closed by authorized personnel. A lock that cannot be opened should be removed immediately and replaced with a working DOD-approved lock. An inquiry should be made to determine whether an apparent substitution of the lock was made in error or as an attempt to create a "trap door" through which unauthorized persons could ingress or egress from a DOD facility.

KEY LOCKS

8-25. Key locks consist of, but are not limited to, the following:

- Cylindrical locksets (see figure 8-1) are often called key-in-knob or key-in-lever locks. They are normally used to secure offices and storerooms. The locking cylinder located in the center of the doorknob distinguishes these locks. Some cylindrical locksets have keyways in each of the opposing knobs that require a key on either side to lock and unlock them. Others unlock with a key, but may be locked by pushing or rotating a button on the inside knob. These locks are suitable only for very low-security applications. Using these locks may require compensatory measures in the form of additional locks on containers within the room.

Figure 8-1. Cylindrical lockset

- Dead bolt locks are sometimes called tubular dead bolts (see figure 8-2). They are either single- or double-cylinder varieties (see figure 8-3) and are mounted on the door in a manner similar to cylindrical locksets. The primary difference is in the bolt. When the bolt is extended (locked), the dead bolt projects into the doorframe at least 1 inch, and it cannot be forced back (unlocked) by applying pressure to the end of the bolt. The dead bolt lock has the potential for providing acceptable levels of protection for storerooms and other areas where more security is desired. It is recommended for use in military housing as an effective security measure in the installation's crime prevention program. In situations where there is a window in or adjacent to the door, a double-cylinder dead bolt lock (one that requires a key to open from either side) should be used. U.S. government key-operated, pin-locking dead bolts that project at least 1 inch into the doorframe or tumbler-type padlocks are used to safeguard unclassified, nonsensitive Army supplies and equipment if a lock is required. Selection is based on the value of items protected, mission essentiality, and vulnerability to criminal attack.

Figure 8-2. Single-cylinder dead bolt

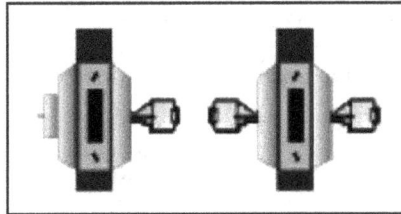

Figure 8-3. Single- and double-cylinder dead bolt

- Mortise locks (see figure 8-4) are so named because the lock case is mortised or recessed into the edge of the door. The most common variety of mortise locks has a doorknob on each side of the door. Entrance doors often have an exterior thumb latch rather than a doorknob. The mortise lock can be locked from inside by means of a thumb turn or by a button. Mortise locks are considered low-security devices since they weaken the door in the mortised area.

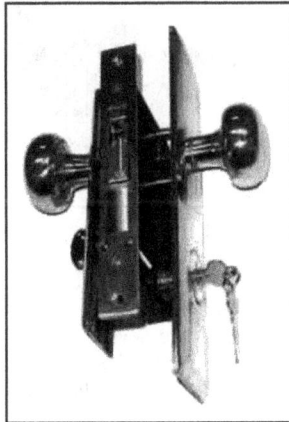

Figure 8-4. Mortise lockset

- Drop bolt locks—often referred to as jimmy-proof locks (see figure 8-5, page 8-6)—are normally used as auxiliary locks similar to dead bolts. Both the drop bolt lock body and the strike have interlocking leaves similar to a door hinge. When closed, locking pins in the lock body drop down into the holes provided in the strike and secure the locking system. Since the lock body and the strike are interconnected with locking pins when closed, the lock essentially becomes a single unit and is extremely difficult to separate.

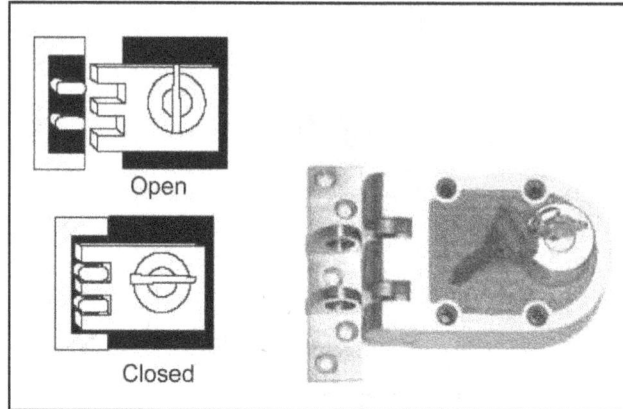

**Figure 8-5. Drop bolt or jimmy-proof lock
in the open and closed position**

- Rim-cylinder locks (see figure 8-6) are mounted to the inside surface of the door and are secured by screws in the door face. These locks are generally used with drop bolt and other surface-mounted locks and latches. They consist of an outer barrel, a cylinder and ring, a tailpiece, a back mounting plate, and two mounting screws. The tailpiece screws are usually scored so that the lock can be tailored to fit varying door thicknesses.

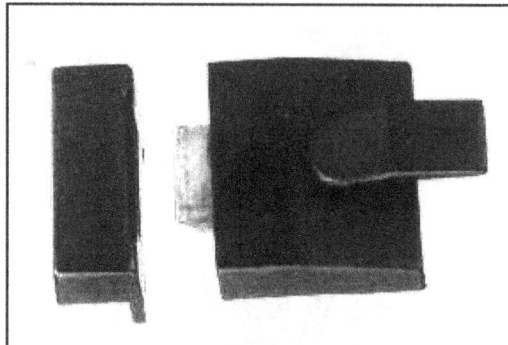

Figure 8-6. Rim-cylinder lock

- Mechanical, push-button combination locks (see figure 8-7) are digital (push buttons numbered 1 through 9) combination door-locking devices used to deny area access to any individual not authorized or cleared for a specific area. These locks are normally used for access control and should be backed up by door-locking devices when the facility is unoccupied.

Figure 8-7. Mechanical push-button combination lock

- Padlocks are detachable locks that are typically used with a hasp. Low-security padlocks (see figure 8-8), sometimes called secondary padlocks, are used to deter unauthorized access, and they provide only minimal resistance to force. Low-security locks are made with hardened steel shackles and body.

Figure 8-8. Low-security padlocks

- High-security padlocks (see figure 8-9, page 8-8) and internal locking device (see figure 8-10, page 8-8) may be used to secure AA&E (see DOD 5100-76-M). High-security padlocks provide the maximum resistance to unauthorized entry when used with a high-security hasp.

Figure 8-9. High-security padlock

Figure 8-10. Internal locking device

8-26. Some locks have interchangeable cores/cylinders (see figure 8-11), which allow the same key system to include a variety of locks. Padlocks, door locks, cabinet locks, and electrical key switches can all be operated by the same key system. Because these cores are removable by a special key, this system allows for rapid re-keying of locks in the event that the key is compromised.

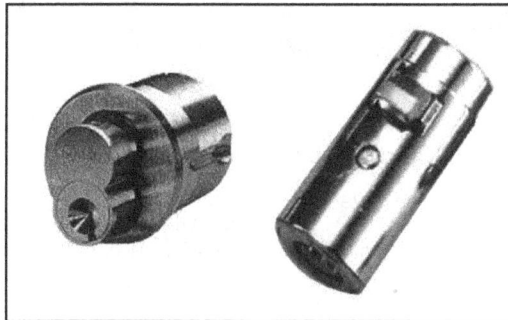

Figure 8-11. Lock cores/cylinders

8-27. Locks are keyed in several different ways:

- When several locks are keyed differently, only the key for that lock will open it.
- When they are keyed alike, one key will open them all.
- Locks that are master-keyed are keyed differently, yet have one key that will open them all. Master keying is done for convenience and represents the controlled loss of security. Master keying is not used unless permitted by regulation.

COMBINATION LOCKS

8-28. Combination locks (see figure 8-12) are available as padlocks or as mounted locks. They range from low- to high-security padlocks with combinations that are either fixed or changeable. Combination locks may be either mechanical or electronic. They are typically used to secure rooms, vaults, or containers. Entering a particular sequence of numbers operates them. When the correct combination is entered, the bolt of the lock is retracted. Combination locks used for securing classified material must meet FS FF-L-2740.

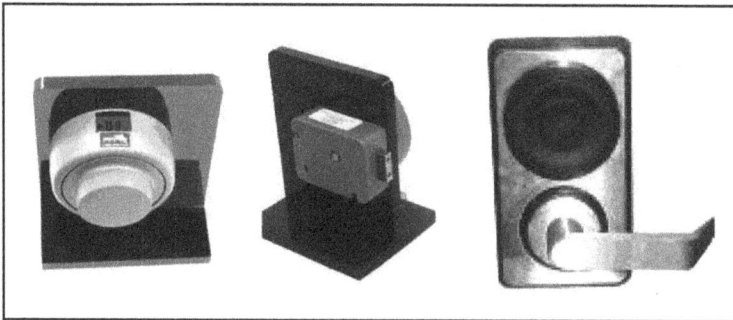

Figure 8-12. Combination locks

SECURITY HINGES AND HASPS

8-29. Depending on the security application being considered, check with the supporting engineering organization for the correct type of hinge or hasp to use. AR 190-11 places more stringent guidelines when using hinges and hasps for AA&E storage. When checking hinges and hasps already in use, ensure that the screws or bolts that fasten the hasp or hinge to the structure are located such that an intruder cannot remove them. Hinges should not be removable from outside. Life and Fire Safety Codes often direct that doors must swing outward, which then places the hinge pins outside. Security hinges are preferred in those cases. If conventional hinges are used, hinge pins must be spot welded, peened, covered, or otherwise secured to prevent removal.

INSTALLATION AND MAINTENANCE OF LOCKS AND KEYS

8-30. USACE is responsible for installing locking devices in newly constructed facilities. Installation-level engineers are responsible for maintaining the locking devices. Physical security personnel must work closely with engineer personnel to ensure that locks meet the standards and are installed according to applicable regulations. One source of assistance and information is the DOD Lock Program Office (see appendix B). The Technical Support Hotline (DSN 551-1212 or commercial [805] 982-1212) is at the Naval Facilities Engineering Services Center, Port Hueneme, California.

8-31. Locks should be inspected and cleaned every 6 months. Corrosion should be removed and the lock lubricated with a nonpetroleum-based product to avoid the collection of dust, dirt, sand, and other contaminants that might render the lock inoperable. If the lock is used for a special purpose (such as arms room or AA&E), the appropriate technical data sheet should be referred to for the correct disassembly and cleaning procedures.

8-32. The deep cuts and sharp angles of a key make it easy for a key to crack if forced or twisted before it is fully inserted into the cylinder of the lock. Key maintenance is performed every time a key is used. If a key does not go in or turn easily in the cylinder of the lock, clean and lubricate the lock. When a key becomes cracked or bent, the key must be taken out of inventory and replaced. The removal of a key also includes removal of the duplicate key and lock from inventory. For assistance in disposing of high-security padlocks, contact the DOD Lock Program Technical Support Hotline.

Chapter 9

Security Forces

One of the most critical components of the physical security system is the dedicated security force. Security forces provide the enforcement element of the physical security program for Army installations and facilities. This force consists of personnel specifically organized, trained, and equipped to protect the command's physical security interests; it is a commander's most effective tool in a comprehensive and integrated physical security program. This chapter describes the security force capabilities available on most Army installations and facilities. Execution of these security activities resides with the designated provost marshal/director of emergency services or security officer. Operational area security, base defense, and perimeter defense are described in Joint Publication (JP) 3-10 and Army FM 3-90.

AUTHORITY AND JURISDICTION

9-1. The Office of the Provost Marshal General establishes policy for developing, training, qualification, and suitability requirements for dedicated security forces (including DA guards, contract security guards, security technicians, and the PSO).

9-2. The 190-series ARs provide realistic guidance and prescribe uniform physical security policies and procedures regarding the employment of security forces. Specific regulations include the following:

- AR 190-11.
- AR 190-12.
- AR 190-13.
- AR 190-14.
- AR 190-16.
- AR 190-17.
- AR 190-51.
- AR 190-54.
- AR 190-56.
- AR 190-58.
- AR 190-59.

9-3. DOD Instruction 1325.06 provides that the commander of a military installation or other military-controlled facility under the jurisdiction of the United States shall prohibit any demonstration or activity on the installation or facility that could result in interference with, or prevention of, orderly accomplishment of the mission of the installation or facility, or present a clear danger to loyalty, discipline, or morale of the troops. It is a crime for any person to enter a military reservation for any purpose prohibited by law or lawful regulations, or for any person to enter or reenter an installation after having been barred by order of the commander under Title 18, U. S. Code (U.S.C.), Section 1382 (reference [c]).

9-4. It is most important that the security officer determine (and instruct the security force in) the extent and limitations of the commander's jurisdiction in the field of law enforcement and investigations. Those jurisdictions include—

- Jurisdiction of place.
  - Whether state or federal law or both are applicable on a military installation or facility depends largely on the nature of jurisdiction over the land involved. The amount of federal jurisdiction may vary between different areas of the installation or facility. The legal formalities of acquiring jurisdiction over land under the control of the Secretary of the Army are accomplished at DA level and according to the provisions of AR 405-20. Information and advice relating to jurisdictional questions should be referred to the local Staff Judge Advocate (SJA).
  - Areas outside of military installations are generally subject to state and local laws; however, there are exceptions. Information and advice in this regard should be obtained through the local SJA.
  - In overseas areas, jurisdiction varies according to the military situation and existing international treaties, contracts, and agreements. Guidance should be obtained in each instance from the commander and the SJA and set forth in appropriate command directives.
- Jurisdiction of personnel.
  - Jurisdiction of personnel generally follows the limitations of jurisdiction of the installation.
  - Military police, Army civilian police, and security guards have jurisdiction and authority to apprehend military members who commit offenses punishable under the Uniform Code of Military Justice (UCMJ) pursuant to AR 600-20. They may apprehend military personnel for all offenses under the UCMJ, military regulations, federal laws and regulations, and state laws, where applicable. Sources that provide apprehension authority are Rules for Courts-Martial (RCM) 302, AR 190-30 at 4-8, AR 195-2 at 3-21, and UCMJ, Article 7. Article 7's apprehension authority applies worldwide. Additional sources describing law enforcement personnel's jurisdiction and authority over military personnel are AR 190-14 and Criminal Investigation Division (CID) Regulation 195-1.
  - Authority for federal civilian employees assigned to security, police, and guard duties is derived from RCM 302 and AR 190-56. Federally employed civilian police and security guards can perform law enforcement and security duties authorized by the installation's commanding officer and are subject to any limitations imposed thereon. These personnel can have no more authority than that possessed by the commander, who is the source of jurisdiction and authority for all other personnel assigned to security-force duties. These personnel may apprehend persons on the installation for felonies, breaches of peace, or those who are a threat to property or welfare (see AR 190-56).
  - The commander is the source of jurisdiction and authority for all other personnel assigned to security-force duties. The provost marshal/director of emergency services, in cooperation with the SJA, issues written instructions for Army civilian police and security guards describing procedures and the limits of their authority. These instructions include the limitations for detention, apprehension, and the use of force. Additionally, instructions for the reaction force and hostage situations are included (see AR 190-56).

TYPES OF SECURITY FORCES

9-5. Security forces normally consist of military police, DA police (job series 0083) and guards (job series 0085), contract security guards, protective services personnel, and MWD teams. These forces are trained, equipped, and employed specifically for law enforcement, personal security, and physical security activities. Their efforts are focused on law enforcement, crime prevention, physical security of critical assets, protection of high-risk personnel, and access control.

9-6. Unit personnel can also be used to secure restricted areas, MEVA, or critical assets during periods of increased threat or when security systems temporarily fail.

9-7.   Military police forces perform law enforcement and security duties that require specialized training. Specific military police duties include—

- Law enforcement.
- Police intelligence operations.
- Area security.
- Detainee and confinement operations.
- Civil disturbance operations.
- Critical asset security.
- Security of restricted areas.
- Supervisory or joint partnership roles with other military, DOD, or contract security personnel.
- Training of HN police and security forces.
- Monitoring of, and responding to, intrusion alarms.

9-8.   Forces that respond to major threats on military installations are grouped in the following categories:

- Emergency responders.
- Special reaction teams (SRTs).
- Other response forces.

9-9.   Emergency responders provide basic capabilities to installations on a day-to-day basis regardless of FPCON levels. Many of these forces are available 24/7. Emergency responders responsible for law enforcement and security normally fall under the command and control of the designated provost marshal/director of emergency services. On most installations, first responders include—

- Military police.
- DA guards.
- Security police.
- Fire department/hazardous material (HAZMAT) personnel.
- MWD teams.
- Emergency medical services personnel.
- Explosive ordnance disposal personnel.
- United States Army Criminal Investigation Command (USACIDC) criminal investigators.

9-10. The SRT is the Army installation commander's most lethal "full-time" response force. An SRT is an integral part of the commander's antiterrorism and physical security program and is the principal response force in case of a major disruption or a special threat situation. Commanders may resource the SRT through a full-time team or memorandum of agreement with a nearby base or civilian police agency. AR 190-58 and FM 3-19.11 (restricted manual) provide guidance for SRT.

9-11. Other response forces may be a designated mobile force with appropriate fire support to defeat level II threats. It usually consists of military police forces supported by available fire support and Army aviation assets. The normal composition is a platoon- or company-size force. If military police elements are temporarily or permanently unavailable in sufficient strength, the commander should designate alternate response forces, such as engineer, chemical, transiting combat units, elements of the reserves, or HN assets. FM 3-90 describes procedures for base defense response force operations.

9-12. Response to threats begins immediately upon detection and is designed to—

- Stop further intrusion by the threat at the greatest distance possible from protected assets.
- Slow the rate of advance toward the protected asset as much as possible.
- Facilitate the evacuation of the protected asset to safe areas.
- Secure the protected asset and contain the threat.
- Contain the threat, prevent additional hostile resources from arriving, and prepare to apprehend the threat and relieve the protected asset.

MILITARY WORKING DOGS

9-13. MWD teams provide a valuable asset to physical security efforts. The dog's sight, smell, and hearing abilities enhance detection capabilities and provide a physical and psychological deterrent to threats. MWD teams are a key resource for explosive detection, search and rescue, narcotics detection, and security patrol operations.

9-14. Specialized search dogs are trained for route, area, building, and vehicle search. These highly trained dogs search for and detect firearms, ammunition, explosives, and other materials used in bomb making. Other MWD capabilities include the following:

- Customs enforcement.
- Suspicious package response.
- Protective services operations.

9-15. In security operations, patrol explosive detection dogs and patrol narcotic detection dogs may be used during both day and night operations. The patrol dog's superior detection ability is especially useful at night or during periods of limited visibility. Patrol dogs can detect a fleeing person and, if necessary, pursue, attack, and hold the person. Employed in a downwind, blocking force dogs can find, and aid in the capture of, intruders or saboteurs, or they can operate in the lead position during response force sweeps.

9-16. Dogs are a valuable adjunct for security operations when they are used for guarding. MWD teams offer a real, and a psychological, deterrent against escape attempts. At ACPs or dismount points, dogs can guard persons during identification checks and deter attempts to gain unauthorized access through force. Other employment considerations include perimeter patrolling, area and route security, and clearing buildings.

9-17. When MWD teams are employed, they take part in all phases of the security mission. The handler recommends ways to use the MWD team. Normally, a dog works best when placed to take advantage of odors carried on the wind. When there is little or no wind, a dog can detect intruders up to 200 meters away using its senses of smell, hearing, and sight. In unfavorable wind conditions, a dog can still detect by sound and sight. But a dog's capabilities are reduced by—

- Noise.
- Movement.
- Smoke.
- Dust.
- Dense undergrowth.
- Heavily wooded areas.
- Jungle growth.

9-18. Petroleum, oil, and lubricants (POL) can damage paws and the dog's sense of smell. Work near POL points must be infrequent and brief. Chemical agents also limit the use of dogs because there are no protective devices for dogs.

9-19. Whenever possible, an MWD team rehearses with team or patrol members so that everyone can get used to working with the dog. Team members also must know what to do if a handler is seriously wounded or killed. A dog that has worked closely with a team and has developed a tolerance for one or more of the members will usually allow one of them to return it to the kennel. However, a dog may not allow anyone near its handler. In this case, other handlers may have to be called on to assist.

9-20. Dogs are useful at posts often secured only in periods of high threat or where occasional random posting is needed during rain, fog, and the like. But locations and limits must be adjusted for factors that affect a dog's ability to see, hear, and smell. For example, lights can cause a dog to rely more on sight than on its other senses. MWD teams operating in lighted areas should patrol varied routes, remain in shadows, or stand stationary in concealed downwind positions as needed. Varied posting of a team increases deterrence by avoiding a set patrol pattern.

9-21. Posting a team inside or outside a fence depends on the purpose of the security—protection of resources or capture of intruders. Table 9-1 provides employment considerations for MWD teams. For additional information, see FM 3-19.17.

Table 9-1. How fences affect military working dog teams

If a dog is positioned—	Team can—	Team cannot—
Inside a fenced area	Patrol close to critical asset. Check critical asset frequently. Respond and assess an activated interior alarm system.	Follow a departing intruder. Resist distraction of a decoy upwind of fence.
Outside a fenced area	Move more easily to work the wind and follow alert to the source. Respond and assess an activated exterior alarm system.	Respond quickly to problem inside fence. Resist following decoy upwind to its source.

ORGANIZATION AND EMPLOYMENT OF SECURITY FORCES

9-22. The organization of a security force will vary, depending on circumstances and the forces available. Forces may consist of the following or a combination of these three—

- **Mobile patrols**. A mobile detachment dispatched to gather information, respond to an incident, or carry out a security mission.
- **Response force**. A mobile force with appropriate fire support (usually designated by the area commander) to deal with Level II threats. This is normally a military police function.
- **Reserves**. That portion of a force withheld from action or uncommitted to a specific course of action so as to be available for commitment at the decisive moment. Its primary purpose is to retain flexibility throughout an offensive action.

9-23. Security personnel periodically check facilities and areas used to store sensitive or critical items or equipment as directed by a threat and vulnerability analysis. Security patrols, inspections, and checks should be conducted on an irregular basis during nonduty hours to avoid establishing a pattern. Unauthorized personnel detected in restricted areas should be identified, questioned and, if necessary, detained. Security personnel should physically inspect doors, locks, and windows on all storage structures and critical facilities in their patrol areas of responsibility.

9-24. Security forces physically man ACPs to provide the human capability to interact with people passing through the control points. They serve as a visible barrier or deterrent and a human intelligence sensor. These forces operate and monitor various surveillance and detection equipment, conduct on-the-spot assessment as part of the initial detection process, and provide the initial response to an incident at control points.

9-25. Written reports or journals are required for security activities. Either the security force's supervisor or the personnel at the security post should prepare these. These reports should record all activities, actions, and visits at the security post.

9-26. It should be strongly emphasized that security personnel will be used for security duties only and should not be given other routine functions, except as directed by the commander or his representative. Security personnel should remain alert at all times and not be assigned tasks that distract from their primary duties.

9-27. Personnel who are assigned to fixed posts should have a designated method of relief. The security force's shift supervisor should establish a relief schedule according to local policies and the SOP.

9-28. A simple, but effective, plan of operation should be worked out for the security force to respond to emergencies. Practice alarms should be conducted frequently to test the plan's effectiveness. Such plans should be designed to prevent a diversion at one point on the installation—drawing off the guards or distracting their attention from another section of the installation where unauthorized entry may be made. Routes and times for security patrols should be varied at frequent intervals to preclude establishing a routine that may be observed by potential intruders.

SECURITY FORCE PLANS AND ORDERS

9-29. Instructions to the security force should be issued in writing and included in the physical security plan (see appendix A). These instructions are normally in the form of general, special, or temporary orders. They should be carefully and clearly worded and include all phases of each assignment. Instructions should be reviewed annually to ensure that they are current. Categories of instructions may include the following:

- **General orders**. Orders that concern the security force as a whole and are applicable at all posts and patrols.
- **Special orders**. Orders that pertain to a permanent post or patrol. Each permanent post or patrol should have special orders issued concerning the location, duties, hours manned, arms, ammunition, and other equipment required and the instructions for using force (lethal and nonlethal) in enforcement and apprehension activities.
- **Temporary orders**. Orders that are issued for a short period and cover a special or temporary situation. If it can be predetermined, such orders should indicate the period of time for which they are valid.

9-30. A security-force SOP that outlines policies, organization, authority, functions, and other required information should be prepared for required reading. Each security-force member is responsible for full knowledge and understanding of the contents of the SOP. Each installation provost marshal, security officer, or chief of a guard force should conduct periodic inspections and tests to determine each individual's degree of understanding of these instructions. Instructions should be provided in writing regarding the safeguarding and control of the SOP. Its contents may not be classified; however, the information could assist an intruder in breaching security.

SECURITY FORCE TRAINING REQUIREMENTS

9-31. The extent and type of training required for security forces will vary according to the mission, vulnerability, size, and other factors affecting a particular installation or facility. The training program's objective is to ensure that all personnel are able to perform routine and emergency duties competently and efficiently. AR 190-56 outlines security and guard force training. Security forces assigned to protect chemical and biological agents and nuclear weapons must meet the training and qualification standards of the Personnel Reliability Program (see AR 190-59).

9-32. All personnel assigned duties with a security force should receive training in the following areas:

- Use of force and ROE.
- FPCON and RAMs.
- Weapons training, qualification, and safety procedures.
- Authority and jurisdiction.
- Search and seizure.
- Nonlethal weapons policy and employment.
- General and special orders.
- HN culture, customs, and courtesies.
- Self-protection measures (mortar/missile attack, IED, chemical attack, conventional attack).
- Countersurveillance measures.
- Emergency alert and notification procedures.

9-33. AR 190-14 encourages the use of nonlethal devices for law enforcement and security personnel. Commanders should ensure that all security personnel are properly trained and certified on nonlethal devices (see FM 3-19.15). The Army proponent for nonlethal weapons policy is Office of the Provost Marshal General. All questions regarding nonlethal weapons policy, both tactical and nontactical, should be directed to The Office of the Provost Marshal General, Military Police Policy Division, 2800 Army Pentagon, Washington, DC 20310-2800.

CALCULATING PERSONNEL REQUIREMENTS

9-34. A formula can be developed on a standard computer spreadsheet that will automatically calculate security personnel requirements.

9-35. The formula is (*number of personnel commitment [times] x total number of days scheduled [divided]/by actual number of days worked [equals] = personnel requirement*). Example: The 24-hour commitment is 100 personnel to work 5 days on and 2 days off. The total number of days on the schedule would be 7 and the actual days worked would be 5 (100 x 7/5 = 140). This requires 140 personnel to fill a commitment of 100 and maintain a 5-days-on and 2-days-off schedule.

MANPOWER CAPABILITY

9-36. When calculating manpower capability, the formula is (*available personnel [times] x actual number of days worked [divided] / by total number of days on schedule [equal] = manpower capability*). Example: There are 100 personnel available to work a 5-days-on and 2-days-off schedule. The actual days worked would be 5 and the total number of days on the schedule would be 7 (100 x 5 / 7 = 71.43 or 71 positions). The results must be rounded down. Since these are strictly mathematical calculations, it is imperative to plan for a 10-percent cushion to account for emergencies, schools, leave, injury, and unexpected illnesses.

This page intentionally left blank.

Chapter 10

Physical Security for In-Transit Forces

The terrorist threat remains one of our nation's most pervasive challenges. History has shown that DOD personnel, facilities, and activities make high-value terrorist targets, and no change is predicted for the near future. Irregular threats use terrorism, insurgency, and guerrilla warfare to interdict U.S. forces that are attempting to enter foreign areas of crisis. These areas are often characterized by the presence of enemies, adversaries, supporters, and neutrals all intermixed with no easy method to distinguish one from another. Commanders must maintain the ability to deploy quickly with little notice, shape conditions in the crisis area, and operate immediately on arrival. In-transit forces confront unique vulnerabilities while traveling great distances to conduct operations. Commanders of U.S. forces always remain responsible for the protection of Soldiers and resources, regardless of location. They protect their forces by identifying the hazards, analyzing the risks, and implementing control measures to mitigate, neutralize, or eliminate hazards and threats (see FM 3-37).

RISK MANAGEMENT FOR DEPLOYING FORCES

10-1. Deploying commanders use a risk management approach in determining which protection measures are appropriate to reduce risk and vulnerability to acceptable levels. Composite risk management is the Army's primary decisionmaking process for identifying hazards and controlling risks across the full spectrum of Army missions, functions, and operations.

10-2. Composite risk management is a decisionmaking process used to mitigate risks associated with all hazards that have the potential to injure or kill personnel, damage or destroy equipment, or otherwise impact mission effectiveness.

10-3. Composite risk management uses a five-step process that serves to subjectively quantify probability and severity of a hazard or threat through the use of the Army risk assessment process (see FM 5-19). The five-step process includes the following:

- **Step 1**. Identify the hazards.
- **Step 2**. Assess hazards to determine risk.
- **Step 3**. Develop controls and make risk decisions.
- **Step 4**. Implement controls.
- **Step 5**. Supervise and evaluate.

10-4. Commanders and staff use the composite risk management process to develop physical security measures designed to protect in-transit personnel and equipment. These procedures should be included in the unit's deployment SOP. Security measures should be tailored to local conditions and include use of force, ROE, billeting security, and security procedures for in-transit aircraft, ship, and ground transportation.

10-5. Figure 10-1, page 10-2, illustrates the five-step composite risk management process.

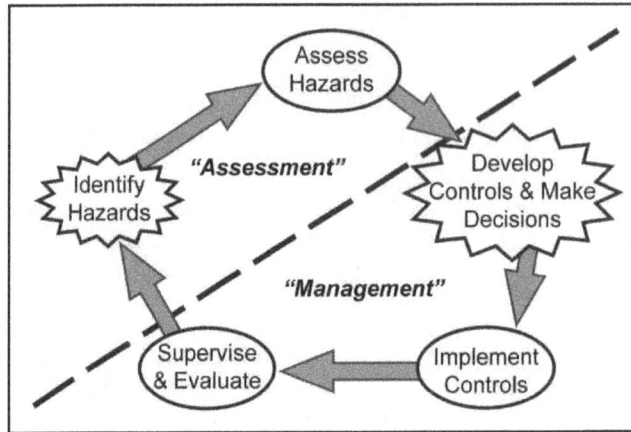

Figure 10-1. Composite risk management process

IDENTIFY THE HAZARDS

10-6. A hazard is a condition with the potential to cause injury, illness, or death of personnel; damage to or loss of equipment or property; or mission degradation. A hazard may also be a situation or event that can result in degradation of capabilities or mission failure. Hazards exist in all environments; however, in-transit forces are especially vulnerable.

10-7. Commanders identify and evaluate potential hazards on the basis of the factors of METT-TC. While the composite risk management is used to identify and reduce all hazards, this discussion focuses the five-step process for terrorist threats against in-transit forces.

10-8. For deploying forces, terrorist threats are among the most catastrophic. To identify potential terrorist threats, commanders should assess factors such as capabilities, intentions, and past activities of known terrorist groups. These assessments represent a systematic approach to identifying potential threats, understanding their tactics, and recognizing indicators of eminent danger before they materialize.

ASSESS THE HAZARDS

10-9. This process is systematic in nature and uses charts, codes, and numbers to present a methodology to assess probability and severity to obtain a standardized level of risk. The five-step composite risk management process is a method for expressing and depicting a normally intuitive and experience-based thought process.

10-10. During the terrorist threat assessment, consider the probability of a terrorist attack in the region, the operational area, and lodgments and the impact of such an attack on the mission, capability, personnel, and equipment.

10-11. Geographic combatant commanders provide threat planning information to deploying units to enable them to perform risk management and develop protection plans. Deploying units traditionally focus physical security efforts primarily on their deployment operational area. Before arriving in an overseas region, commanders are required to submit protection plans to the geographic combatant commander responsible for protection of all military forces in their region. The procedures in the deploying unit's plans must match the guidance developed by the geographic combatant commander, who coordinates and approves the individual plans. This allows the commander to ensure that a unit's plan takes into account all current threats that could affect the mission and to accept or mitigate any security risks that arise.

10-12.   When assessments are not site-specific, they may not adequately capture all emerging threats. This is true when information is only based on higher-level regional assessments that do not focus on the individual rail, sea, or airport facility. Regional assessments often provide a broad view of the threat environment but do not provide site-specific threat information.

10-13.   Commanders assess threats and associated risk by assessing the probability of the event or occurrence; estimating the expected result or severity of an event or occurrence; and determining the specific level of risk for a given probability and severity, using the standard risk assessment matrix. Table 10-1 illustrates the risk assessment matrix.

Table 10-1. Risk assessment matrix

Risk Assessment Matrix						
		Probability				
Severity		Frequent A	Likely B	Occasional C	Seldom D	Unlikely E
Catastrophic	I	E	E	H	H	M
Critical	II	E	H	H	M	L
Marginal	III	H	M	M	L	L
Negligible	IV	M	L	L	L	L

Legend:

E-Extremely High Risk: Loss of ability to accomplish the mission if threats occur during mission. A frequent or likely probability of catastrophic loss (IA or IB) or frequent probability of critical loss (IIA) exists.

H-High Risk: Significant degradation of mission capabilities in terms of the required mission standard, inability to accomplish all parts of the mission, or inability to complete the mission to standard if threats occur during the mission. Occasional-to-seldom probability of catastrophic loss (IC or ID) exists. A likely-to-occasional probability exists of a critical loss (IIB or IIC) occurring. Frequent probability of marginal losses (IIIA) exists.

M-Moderate Risk: Expected degraded mission capabilities in terms of the required mission standard will have a reduced mission capability if threats occur during mission. An unlikely probability of catastrophic loss (IE) exists. The probability of a critical loss is seldom (IID). Marginal losses occur with a likely or occasional probability (IIIB or IIIC). A frequent probability of negligible (IVA) losses exists.

L-Low Risk: Expected losses have little or no impact on accomplishing the mission. The probability of critical loss is unlikely (IIE), while that of marginal loss is seldom (IIID) or unlikely (IIIE). The probability of a negligible loss is likely or less (IVB through IVE).

10-14.   Units assess hazards to determine their own vulnerability before deployment. These assessments must be conducted sufficiently in advance of deployments to allow for the development of security procedures, acquisition of necessary materials, obtainment of focused intelligence, coordination of necessary security augmentation forces, and request of necessary HN support. Assessments must address hazards and threats to rest areas, refueling locations, and movement routes.

DEVELOP CONTROLS AND MAKE RISK DECISIONS

10-15.   The process of developing and applying controls and reassessing risk continues until an acceptable level of risk is achieved or until all risks are reduced to a level where benefits outweigh the potential cost.

10-16. Assessments should provide the commander a baseline to implement appropriate protection measures to reduce and/or mitigate risk. Predeployment assessments must occur in a timely manner and should be incorporated in predeployment planning and training. These assessments will assist commanders in updating operational area-specific training and in obtaining necessary physical security materials and equipment to implement protective measures.

10-17. After assessing the terrorist threat, the commander develops physical security plans for self-protection while in transit. Although emphasis must be on movements through high-threat areas, commanders should not discount appropriate security measures for movements in lower-threat areas. Physical security plans for movements through high-threat areas must be completed and approved by the appropriate geographic combatant commander.

10-18. The key to providing protection is to design the physical security program to provide layered protection in all directions. Programs should emphasize the use of electronic early warning sensors, access control measures, and sufficient security forces to patrol, guard, and respond to unauthorized acts.

IMPLEMENTING CONTROLS

10-19. Leaders and staffs ensure that controls are integrated into SOPs, written and verbal orders, mission briefings, and staff estimates. The critical check for this step is to ensure that controls are converted into clear and simple execution orders. Units must prepare a unit movement operations SOP. Each deployment requires a separate SOP tailored to the specific operational area.

10-20. Commanders must implement appropriate protection measures to reduce risk and vulnerability. Advanced or onboard security augmentation should be considered for travel through high-threat areas. Equipment such as electronic surveillance cameras and monitors, explosive detection devices, and blast mitigation equipment can significantly enhance a transiting unit's protection posture against hazards and threats. Commanders should consider commercial-off-the-shelf or government-off-the-shelf products to meet near-term protection requirements. Funds for these items are requested through the Combating Terrorism Readiness Initiatives Fund (CBT–RIF).

10-21. Authorized activities supported by CBT–RIF funds include—
- Procurement and maintenance of physical security equipment.
- Improvement of physical security sites.
- Under extraordinary circumstances:
  - Physical security management planning.
  - Procurement and support of security forces and security technicians.
  - Security reviews and investigations and vulnerability assessments.
  - Any other activity relating to physical security.

SUPERVISE AND EVALUATE

10-22. Like other steps of the composite risk management process, supervision and evaluation must occur throughout all phases of any operation or activity. This continuous process provides the ability to identify weaknesses and to make changes or adjustments to controls based on performance, changing situations, conditions, or events.

10-23. Once controls are implemented, the commander enforces protection procedures and evaluates their effectiveness. The PSO conducts inspections, surveys, and security assessments to identify protection gaps. If a security shortfall exists, the PSO recommends solutions to the commander. Physical security measures are scalable and designed to increase protection to meet fluctuating demands of changing threat levels.

OPERATIONS SECURITY

10-24. Many potential adversaries consider in-transit forces, logistics units, and lodgments to be prime targets. Probable targets where these forces are normally located include ports, transfer points, and along main roads and inland waterways. These areas are all supported and used by units moving in and out of operational areas. An adversary may employ hazards or threats to disrupt activities (even during periods not associated with combat) using ambushes, snipers, raids, or sabotage.

10-25. Operations security is an integral part of planning for in-transit security. Throughout the planning, preparation, and execution phases of a deployment, every effort must be made to maintain security. Commanders reduce risk and protect their forces by developing effective operations security protective measures using a four-step planning sequence that includes the following:

- Determine enemy capabilities for obtaining information about in-transit operations.
- Determine what information obtained by the threat can compromise the operation.
- Determine which actions taken by the unit, if known and analyzed by the threat, can give the adversary the information needed.
- Determine what protective measures are necessary and where they must be implemented to maximize operations security.

10-26. Commanders employ physical security measures such as access control, fences, guards, electronic countersurveillance, and security patrols to prevent unauthorized access to personnel, equipment, installations, facilities, and operations.

UNIT MOVEMENT ROLES AND RESPONSIBILITIES

10-27. Unit movement operations involve the command's staff expertise in personnel, intelligence, operations, and logistics. At the battalion and brigade levels, staff responsibility for movement operations resides with the operations staff officer (S-3) and is executed in coordination with the logistics staff officer (S-4). Higher headquarters operations and intelligence staff conduct mission analysis and receive the commander's intent for accomplishing the mission. The next step is to produce several courses of action to accomplish the mission. These courses of action may involve several task organizations and usually address limitations in transportation capability to support the mission. A course of action and task organization are selected that start the unit movement planning sequence. Staff planners need to translate operational mission requirements into detailed and realistic unit movement plans. This translation must occur in a short timeframe and must be able to capture continuous changes based on the current tactical situation. This process involves task organizing, echeloning, tailoring, and movement.

10-28. Unit equipment must be safeguarded according to governing regulations and SOPs while it is being transported to, and staged at, installations, marshaling areas, and port of embarkation (POE). Beyond usual unit safeguarding provisions, certain cargo categories require care while in-transit, and some special cargo categories require extraordinary protection and monitoring while in-transit. Units must comply with the provisions of AR 190-11 (also see DOD 5100.76-M). These regulations assign various levels of required protection and monitoring to material based on categories of risk. Measures of protection and monitoring range from continuous surveillance to a simple seal used in shipping.

10-29. Army units deploy personnel, supplies, and equipment by sea through a port that is commanded or contracted by Surface Deployment and Distribution Command (SDDC). Before being loaded on vessels, unit personnel, supplies, and equipment are held in the port staging area to prepare for shipment. Before moving to the port staging area, the unit, its supplies, and equipment may be assembled in a marshaling area. There is a distinction between the two areas, although they serve much the same purpose. In a marshaling area, the owning command retains responsibility for physical security and accountability for the shipment. Once in the staging area, the port commander assumes custody of equipment and supplies.

10-30. Rail movement may require rail guards, while shipments by sea may require personnel assigned as supercargo. Supercargo personnel are Soldiers designated by a deploying unit to supervise, guard, and maintain unit cargo aboard the vessel during surge mode operations. The supercargo assignments also involve security of personal weapons, ammunition, and classified material.

RAIL GUARDS

10-31. The deploying unit commander makes the final determination based on security requirements and coordinates with the installation transportation officer (ITO) in the continental United States (CONUS) or the unit movement coordinator outside the continental United States (OCONUS) and authorized railroad representatives on guard/escort matters. Guards/escorts are armed at the installation commander's discretion. When armed guards are used, all participating railroads must be notified. All armed guards must be familiar with the ROE and trained in the use of force.

10-32. Cargo guards or escorts maintain surveillance over the military equipment during the journey and notify railroad personnel of any problems. The rail cargo escorts help railroad personnel protect and maintain security of Army equipment loaded aboard trains and protect U.S. Army interests. When OCONUS, HN support is used when appropriate. A copy of the trip itinerary is given to the cargo escort supervisor and includes the rail routing by specific rail companies, interchange points, and stop-off points within a given rail line. The escorts are given portable radios to maintain communication with escort supervisors and other escorts. Escorts are instructed on locomotive and railroad safety. Additionally, escorts will be briefed on ROE before the train leaves the station.

SUPERCARGOES

10-33. Supercargoes are unit personnel designated on orders to accompany, secure, and maintain unit cargo aboard ships. Supercargoes are the deploying unit commander's onboard representatives during the movement of unit equipment on a ship. They perform liaison during cargo reception at the seaport of embarkation (SPOE), shipload and discharge operations, and seaport of debarkation (SPOD) port clearance operations.

10-34. Upon arrival at the SPOE, supercargoes are under the operational control (OPCON) of the port commander. While aboard a ship, the supercargoes are under the command and control of the vessel's captain or first mate. Upon arrival at the SPOD, supercargoes are under the OPCON of the port commander. Supercargoes are normally released to the unit on completion of port clearance operations.

10-35. Unit commanders recommend the composition of supercargoes based on several factors, including the amount and types of equipment loaded aboard the ship and the number of units with equipment on the ship.

IN-PORT CARGO

10-36. Securing DOD facilities located astride waterways is an especially challenging task. Like airfield security, port security begins with the basic problem of securing the facility and assets housed or contained therein by erecting appropriate perimeters and installing physical security devices to detect attempted or successful perimeter penetrations.

10-37. Ports and harbors are prime targets for enemy and criminal activities. Perimeter areas of these facilities are more vulnerable because of the extensive distance and exposed beach or pier areas. Terminal areas may include fully developed piers and warehouses or may be an unimproved beach where logistics-over-the-shore, roll-on/roll-off, or port discharge operations are conducted.

10-38. The problem of securing the waterside of a DOD installation is equally challenging because there is substantial difficulty in distinguishing friend or foe even under the best of circumstances. Also rules of navigation make strict enforcement of perimeters difficult, as these rules allow for emergencies, tidal and wind action, and even errors by eager but less-skilled operators of vessels or craft. Background activity outside the perimeter of a DOD installation makes detection, classification, and identification of hazards and threats difficult.

10-39. Securing ports against terrorist attack is further complicated by two factors:
- The quantity of materiel in-transit to and from port areas is enormous.
- The quantities are so large that it is physically impossible to inspect each container or bulk cargo shipment for weapons, explosives, or other terrorist contraband.

10-40. Hence, waterside security must include the establishment of a security perimeter at the water's edge to detect presence of hazards and threats. The security perimeter must be extended into the water if threats are assessed as having the capability to launch attacks using standoff weapons from boats or other craft.

10-41. External surveillance must monitor traffic on the surface of the water adjacent to the facility, extending from the barrier to a range exceeding that of identified terrorist threats. The outer limit of the surveillance area extends well beyond the estimated outer range of most waterborne weapons. A security zone is established in the surveillance area extending from the high-water mark to a distance at least 1,000 meters from shore, if possible. In some port areas the security zone may be constrained, while in other areas the security zone may be extended farther, especially if the threat includes longer-range surveillance equipment. Within the security zone exist two other zones. They are—

- **A warning zone.** Security forces notify vessels, craft, and swimmers that they are entering restricted waters and should alter their course. Security forces may stop and search intruders if necessary.
- **A reaction zone.** Security forces should prevent the entry of all unauthorized craft or vessels into this zone. Here, aggressive actions may be undertaken to isolate, delay, and resolve potential threats to DOD assets from waterside threat action. The tactical response force (in this case, a boat) may be used. In addition to organic security, forces may be provided by HN or contracted personnel.

10-42. If a military police unit must provide security for cargo in a port, the main effort is to provide security from the perimeter of the port outward. Security measures focus on aggressive patrolling to detect, report and, if need be, combat hazards and threats. Measures may include—

- Conducting route and area reconnaissance patrols.
- Developing police intelligence in the operational area.
- Controlling traffic in the area surrounding the port.
- Conducting mounted or dismounted patrols (with MWDs, if available) around the port's perimeter.
- Establishing an access control/identification section.
- Watching for diversions of supplies out of the port.
- Providing a response force to react to incidents inside the port's perimeter.
- Providing observation and early warning of threat ground and air attacks.

10-43. When providing security for cargo, the focus is on providing a security overwatch for the cargo as it moves from the port to the operational area. Inside a port's perimeter, access to cargo is limited by—

- Operating random mounted or dismounted patrols (with MWDs, if available).
- Using combined patrols as a response force for incidents inside the perimeter.
- Controlling access to the most restricted areas.

10-44. On occasion, the military police may have to safeguard highly critical cargo inside a port's perimeter. The type and degree of security provided is based on logistical security information. Some examples are the—

- Types and values of the cargo stored.
- Vulnerability of the cargo to a land threat.
- Likelihood of theft, diversion, pilferage, or sabotage by military personnel, local workers, black marketers, or enemy agents.
- Location and nature of the port facilities.
- HN agreements.
- Degree of entrance and exit controls.

10-45. Safeguarding the most critical cargo waiting to be transferred to land transport is the priority. The following measures help to safeguard stored cargo:

- Establishing access control procedures.
- Searching bundles and packages being taken from the area.
- Examining trip tickets and documentation of cargo vehicles.
- Installing security lighting.
- Using electronic surveillance devices.

10-46. If the restricted area is a pier or other maritime environment, access from the water must be controlled as well as from the land. Entry on the landward side of a pier can be limited with fencing, pass control, and aggressive patrolling, but the part of the pier that protrudes over the water is accessible from the sides and from below.

10-47. Similarly, intrusion detection devices cannot be easily installed on most barriers used to establish boundaries of a DOD installation or facility when those boundaries extend from several hundred meters to more than 1,000 meters into the water. Some intrusion detection devices can be mounted on fixed installations that extend into the water—such as wharves, piers, or navigation aid platforms. The fact that the barriers have to work on the surface and beneath the surface against a wide variety of threats, without harming benign intrusions, complicates the design and implementation of barriers.

10-48. Methods for securing the pier along its water boundaries include—
- Patrols (both walking on the pier and in small boats).
- Protective lighting.
- Nets (where allowed).
- Buoys or floats.
- Anchored or pile-mounted navigational aids and signaling devices.
- Log booms, blue barrels, 55-gallon drums, and Dunlop boat barriers.
- Barges.
- Gig boats, whaleboats, and other small workboats at anchor.

10-49. The Coast Guard or the Navy may already be performing security in the waters surrounding the pier, which requires the commander to coordinate with those respective elements.

10-50. Once boundaries are established, they can be used to provide areas of operation for floating security patrols as well as contact and escort services and response force activities. It must be emphasized that rules of navigation allow for inadvertent and innocent penetration of certain types of barriers—as may occur with small craft engine failure, sail boats and, in some waters, inexperienced sailors whose enthusiasm for water sports exceeds their navigational and operational skill.

10-51. While most of the barriers described above will stop or impede access to facilities from boats or swimmers, nets are among the most effective. Well-marked, partially submerged objects are also effective; however, there may be legal prohibitions against placing barriers that may constitute a hazard to navigation. These barriers should be placed only after coordination with, and approval by, the appropriate legal and HN authorities. Sometimes it is best to close off the waterside of a pier. A floating boom will keep small boats out. Suspending a cable or a chain-link net from the bottom of the boom will deny access underwater.

10-52. To keep the cargo secured while transferring from one transport method to another, the traffic moving in and out of cargo-handling areas must be controlled. Military police or other security forces can—
- Set up a single access control point.
- Erect field-expedient barriers. Truck trailers or other large vehicles can be used to constrict the traffic flow if permanent barriers are not in place.
- Limit entry to mission-essential personnel, vehicles, and equipment (as designated by the port authority).

10-53. A holding area should be provided if vehicles other than cargo vehicles use the gates. Cargo vehicles can pull into the holding area while they are being checked. The holding area should be large enough to handle the volume and size of traffic. To facilitate cargo checking, use a wooden deck or platform at, or slightly higher than, the level of the truck bed. The platform must be at least as long as the vehicle (such as an empty flatbed trailer). Such a platform makes it quicker and easier to observe and check cargo.

10-54. Cargo is less likely to be diverted if a close watch is kept on cargo documentation and container safety. Containerized cargo is less likely to be stolen or sabotaged. However, containers must be watched closely as they are filled and sealed. Cargo can be pilfered before the seal is applied. An unsealed container can be moved to a stacking area, or someone may apply a false seal, break the seal later, remove the cargo, and then apply a legitimate seal.

10-55. At access control points—

- Inbound and outbound containers should be inspected for signs of damage or nonserviceable conditions.
- Containers must be inspected for the presence of seals or locks and hinges. Their serviceability should also be checked.
- The document's transport number, container number, and seal number should be checked to ensure that they match those numbers on the transportation control-and-movement document. (Check the seals by handling them, not simply by a visual check.)
- Containers with valid documents only should be allowed to pass inbound or outbound through the control point.

RAIL CARGO

10-56. Installation commanders are responsible for securing railways within the boundary of the installation and off-post railway sections when they are used for military purposes. The latter is inherent in the commander's in-transit cargo responsibilities. Railways may be used to move military personnel and equipment during deployments and redeployments. It is conceivable that an adversary will make use of any suitable railway service to move about the area, to transport equipment, or hijack military personnel. Thus, it is critical to secure railcars at all times: during loading, stops, and offloading—360-degree security must be provided.

10-57. Incoming railcars to an installation must be inspected. If a car is sealed and is not intended for that installation, the seal must be checked and verified. If the seal has been tampered with or broken, it must be reported to the train commander. Access to the rail yard is closely monitored and controlled.

10-58. Because a train's movement is determined directly by the condition of the tracks, cargo moving by rail is particularly vulnerable to attack. The destruction of switches, signals, or the track may be a delaying harassment, or it could trigger a major catastrophe. Since railroads can be such high-value targets, the commander may task military police or other U.S. forces to provide onboard security for critical cargo.

10-59. Most train crews consist of four or five people who control the train—the engineer, a conductor, a fireman, a senior brakeman, and a brakeman or a flagman. The conductor is the train commander, unless a transportation railway service officer is assigned to the train. The train commander is responsible for the train's operation and security. He makes all decisions affecting the train.

10-60. The security force commander is responsible for the cargo's security. The train crew and the security force watch for and report any discrepancies or interruptions to normal procedures at any time during the movement. Information about the movement is usually sent along the movement route by the chief dispatcher through a telephone circuit.

10-61. A four- to six-person security force is usually enough to secure railway shipments of sensitive freight, but additional security forces may be needed for moving critical cargo. In addition to a military security force, the shipper or loading agency may send specially trained personnel with highly sensitive cargo. The number of military police in a train security force depends on the—

- Sensitivity of the freight.
- Priority of need for the freight.
- Terrain over which the train will pass.
- Length of the train.
- Duration of the trip.
- Degree of threat.

10-62.   Security forces prepare and maintain a record (by car number) of guarded cars in the train. Security forces can ride in—

- A specific car that requires protection.
- The caboose.
- A security-force car. (If only one security car is used, it should be near the center of the train; if more than one is used, cars should be spaced to provide the best protection for the train.)

10-63.   The security force on a train must keep a constant check on car doors, seals, wires, and locks to detect tampering. The following instances must be noted and reported immediately:

- Irregularities in procedures.
- Presence or actions of unauthorized persons.
- Deficiencies or unauthorized acts that occur.

10-64.   When planning rail-cargo security, the time schedule for the rail movement must be obtained. A map reconnaissance of the route should be provided, detailing bridges and tunnels that are especially vulnerable.

10-65.   Security-force actions should be planned at scheduled stops or relief points, and forces should be deployed according to these plans. Locations of military police units and other friendly forces should be plotted along the route, and their radio frequencies and call signs or other contact information should be noted. An intelligence report covering the route should also be obtained. The report should indicate sites where previous attacks occurred, locations where sabotage or attacks may occur, and where thefts or pilferage are likely.

10-66.   The shipper is responsible for the security of all carload freight until it is turned over to the rail operator and the loaded cars are coupled to a locomotive for movement. The shipper or field transportation officer should complete the freight waybill or the government bill of lading. This report shows the car number, a brief description of contents, and the weight of the load, the consignor, the consignee, the origin, and the destination. In addition, it may show special instructions for the movement or security of the car and its contents. Careful documentation is essential for—

- Securing the shipment.
- Locating cars with critical cargo.
- Ensuring that priority movement is authorized.

10-67.   Transportation officers are responsible for the completeness, correctness, and proper handling of waybills. Each car must have a waybill; this allows cars to be detached or left behind if they become defective en route. If this occurs, a team from the security force must remain with the cargo until they are relieved.

10-68.   Railway cars are sealed after loading. A seal shows that a car has been inventoried and inspected. The standard method of sealing a railway boxcar door (in addition to padlocks or wires) is with a soft metal strap or a cable seal that contains a serial number. Maintaining rigid accountability of all seals is necessary to prevent the undetected replacement of an original seal with another. While sealing does not prevent pilferage, a broken seal is a good indicator that the car and its contents have been tampered with.

10-69.   Train security forces or operating crews can easily check the seals on cars when the train stops. Broken seals should be reported immediately to help pinpoint the time and place of a possible theft. When vehicles are shipped by railcar, sensitive and high-value items must not be secured in the vehicles, but shipped by separate containers. These must be locked and sealed and, if possible, placed door to door for additional security.

10-70.   When operations permit, cars containing highly pilferable freight, high-priority cargo, or special shipments are grouped in the train to permit the most economical use of security forces. When flatcars or gondolas are used to transport sensitive or easily pilfered freight, security forces should be placed where they can continuously observe and protect these cars.

10-71. When the train is stopped, security forces should dismount and check both sides of the train, verifying that seals, locks, and wires are intact. They must report a broken seal immediately to help pinpoint the time and place of the theft.

10-72. If the security force is relieved by another security force while en route, a joint inspection of the cars is conducted. The relief force signs the record being kept on the guarded cars. Consignees assume responsibility for the security of loaded freight cars at the time they arrive at their destination. When the trip is complete, the receiver or his agent will inspect the cars. The security force obtains a receipt for the cars, which is then attached to the trip report. The trip report should include—

- Dates and times the trip started and ended.
- Any additional information required by the local SOP or command directive.
- Recommendations for correcting deficiencies or for improving future security on trains.

10-73. Because unloading points are highly vulnerable to pilferage and sabotage, cars should be unloaded as soon as possible to reduce the opportunity for loss. Military police forces are normally not available for the security of freight in railway yards.

AIR MOVEMENTS

10-74. Army units deploy personnel, supplies, and equipment by air through an aerial port of embarkation (APOE) that is generally operated by the Air Force. It may be on an Air National Guard Base or a commercial airfield. All ports must have communications and be able to provide in-transit visibility of unit equipment during this phase of movement. This capability must extend to providing advance arrival information to the aerial port of debarkation (APOD).

10-75. There are distinct differences between an SPOE and an APOE. Most notable is that the APOE uses four separate areas of movement preparation. Personnel, supplies, and equipment go from the marshaling area to an alert holding area, to a call forward area, and finally to a loading ramp area. These latter three areas—the alert holding area, call forward area, and loading ramp area—are used at an APOE instead of the single staging area of an SPOE.

10-76. The marshalling area activities are the responsibility of the deploying unit commander. The primary purpose of a marshaling area is to provide a location near the port complex to assemble personnel, unit supplies, and equipment and make final preparations for air shipment before entering the alert holding area. Unit marshaling areas are used to receive convoys and process vehicles before they are staged for loading. Support installations, area support groups, or other organizations can be tasked to establish a marshaling area. Here, unit equipment is configured for movement before personnel enter the alert holding area. The deploying unit commander may be required to provide security of vehicles and equipment in the marshalling area. The security force should be provided with written guard instructions that address appropriate security-related information to include use of force (see chapter 9).

10-77.   Once the deploying unit moves to the alert holding area, the Air Force is responsible for security measures until the unit is released from the APOD. A notional APOE structure is shown in figure 10-2.

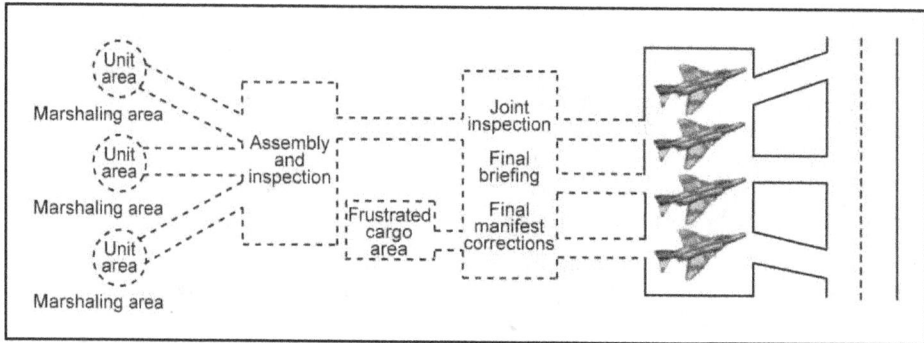

Figure 10-2. Notional aerial port of embarkation

Chapter 11

Resource Management

Physical security costs continue to be one of the commander's single largest budget line items; thus every effort is made to base protection measures on realistic assessments of threats. Commanders must prioritize assets so that security resources can be applied in the most efficient and cost-effective manner. Commanders are continuously challenged to balance resourcing demands with providing quality services and protection to ensure the well-being of Soldiers and their families. As military installations undergo a massive restationing effort and evolve into deployment platforms and sustainment bases, security and protection requirements continue to increase. Defeating hazards and threats from terrorism, biohazards, and information compromise requires full-dimensional protection.

GENERATING REQUIREMENTS

11-1. To assess resource requirements, the development of an executable physical security plan is critical. It is important to identify and document in the plan the required resources needed to protect assets. Given limited resources and budgetary constraints, the plan should provide commanders with effective alternatives. A well-designed, integrated systems approach is essential. A typical physical security systems approach should include resources capable of performing—

- Detection.
- Classification and assessment.
- Delay.
- Communications.
- Response.

11-2. Once the physical security plan is complete, a threat assessment conducted, and critical assets identified, a vulnerability assessment must be done. During vulnerability assessments, a higher headquarters team (joint staff, combatant commander, component command, or Service) provides both procedural and programmatic recommendations to mitigate vulnerabilities and reduce risk. Based on this analysis, the commander, along with a working group, determines whether to adopt these recommendations. Implementing, changing, or adding procedures may or may not mitigate the risk. Since no risk can be reduced to zero, the commander determines if the risk is acceptable and what resources are required.

11-3. Security resource requirements (manpower, operations, and equipment) should be identified for all levels of protection. It is essential that resources are obtained to meet the minimum security requirements. In identifying the resource requirements, it is important that working groups—such as the protection working group—are involved. Working groups should comprise members from all organizations involved in the security plan and program (including the financial manager/resource manager/comptroller). The protection working group members have the input to adequately assess threats, vulnerabilities, critical assets, security program deficiencies/current effectiveness, and risk. See FM 3-37 for additional information regarding the protection working group.

DOCUMENTING RESOURCE REQUIREMENTS

11-4. Formally documenting resource requirements is crucial in defining, prioritizing, and justifying and effectively competing for funding resources. A formal DOD requirements process has been established by the Office of the Secretary of Defense (OSD). The Services, OSD, and joint staff use this methodology to document and prioritize requirements for the Planning, Programming, Budgeting, and Execution System (PPBES) process and the CBT–RIF. The PPBES procedures are described in AR 1-1. General guidelines for obtaining CBT–RIF are described in the following pages.

11-5. Activities/installations/units at the lowest level should document requirements and should forward requirements to higher headquarters. Requirements are annotated using a prescribed format. Spreadsheet formats are available through the Army and higher headquarters security offices. The installation or unit security officer must work closely with the resource manager or financial manager to complete the spreadsheet and provide all the required data. The following information is required for the spreadsheet:

- **Control number.** This is the method used to track and identify the status of numerous unfunded requirements (UFRs). The numbers also allow joint staff, OSD, and the Services to track the history of the initial request from year to year. Once the control number is established, it should not change and should stay with the project until the project is funded. The control number shall consist of four parts: code letter(s) to identify the combatant command, the component, the fiscal year (last two digits of the year) the requirement was initially identified, and a sequence number. For example, the control number P-A-06-0001 is a PACOM (P) Army (A) requirement identified in fiscal year 2006 (06) and is project #1 (0001).
- **Service/agency.** The service/agency responsible for funding the requirement.
- **Component.** The Service component affiliated with the requirement.
- **Location/FPCON.** The location (city and country) of the activity/installation/unit and the FPCON level.
- **Priority.** Prioritize each requirement based on the justification of the threat, vulnerability, criticality, the security plan effectiveness, and the commander's risk according to guidelines (prioritizing requirements). When prioritizing, it is important to consider the short- and long-term effects; affordability and supportability issues; and the cost-benefit impact on life cycle costs, such as manpower and maintenance.
- **Requirement title.** Identify the program requirement. Be as descriptive as possible to avoid confusion with other similarly named requirements (for example, hydraulic barriers versus barriers).
- **Requirement description.** Fully describe the program requirement. The description should include any applicable standards, regulations, and plans on which the requirement is based. Requirements are typically equipment, personnel, or maintenance type.
- **Equipment.** Identify the resource requirement and the description and name with specific quantities and unit price, if applicable.
- **Personnel requirements.** Manpower includes requirements for either guards (contract, military or civilian) or management and planning (for example, PSO, antiterrorism officer).
- **Guards.** Identify the requirement as either contract guards, military or civilian manpower. If contract guards are required to reduce borrowed military manpower, identify the number of borrowed military manpower that the requirement shall reduce and the total borrowed military manpower present. If military manpower is required, identify the number required, officer or enlisted, and associated grades. Provide a brief duty description for each position (such as security guard, security administration personnel). Example: 50 military positions required for security guard positions—patrols, access control—all enlisted personnel, 25 sergeants and 25 staff sergeants. If civilian personnel are required, identify by grade and the number required for each. Provide a brief duty description for each position (such as security guard, security administration personnel). Example: 50 contract guard positions—patrols, access control (10 supervisors, 40 guards).
- **Management and planning.** Identify the requirement as a contractor, military manpower, or civilian. If a contractor is required, identify the number, and provide a brief description of responsibilities. If manpower is required, specify civilian or military, identify the number required, the ranks and grades for each, and provide a brief duty description for each. Examples: 25 junior enlisted security personnel required for badge/administrative duties or 5 training personnel (General Service-4) required to conduct Level-I antiterrorism training.

- **Maintenance requirements.** Identify the item for which maintenance is required and the cost/year. Identify the normal life expectancy of the item, the basis for the replacement, and a projected replacement date.
- **Type integrated vulnerability assessment.** Identify how the requirement was identified and recommended (joint staff integrated vulnerability assessment, Service vulnerability assessment, combatant commander vulnerability assessment, major command vulnerability assessment, self-assessment, security plan development, exercise), and the date (month/year) the assessment was conducted. If the requirement is for additional manpower, include how the manpower position was validated.
- **Justification.** It is important to continuously document and justify requirements in terms of the threat, asset criticality, current security program effectiveness, and vulnerability. The justification is composed of the following four elements: threat assessment, vulnerability assessment, asset criticality assessment, and security plan/program effectiveness. This information and the interrelationship between the categories become the basis for the commander's risk assessment. The ultimate goal is to ensure that appropriate justification is provided to acquire a resource that offers a high-to-moderate degree of protection and provides the capability to meet all or some of the objectives of the security plan/program.
- **Threat.** Both the threat level (high, significant, moderate, and low) and specific threat (such as chemical/biological/radiological/nuclear or IED) should be described for the location or unit requesting the resource. This will give the chain of command insight (based on intelligence information) into the anticipated terrorist's operational capability, intentions, activity, and operating environment and an understanding of the magnitude of the threat.
- **Vulnerability assessment.** Higher headquarters assessment teams assess an organization's current security program and its effectiveness to identify vulnerabilities. These vulnerabilities are typically linked to three areas: construction deficiencies, accessibility, and recognizability. Vulnerabilities need to be described in terms of these three applicable areas. This enables the chain of command to understand the magnitude of the vulnerability and assists in determining the appropriate level of risk. Thoroughly describing the vulnerability is important for lower-threat environments where emphasis and priorities are usually lower than in higher-threat environments.
- **Criticality of assets.** The criticality of assets (personnel, facilities, weapon systems) should be described in terms of importance (asset value), the effect of an incident (ramifications to area/mission), and recovery (time to restore). Describing the criticality of assets in these terms assists in prioritizing resources.
- **Program effectiveness.** Assessing the current security program effectiveness helps determine if there are deficiencies in manpower, policy/procedures/plans, equipment, and training/exercises. Typically, if resources are required, deficiencies are identified in manpower or equipment. These deficiencies need to be described to explain why existing manpower and equipment resources cannot mitigate the risk.
- **Commander's risk assessment.** A commander, with the assistance of staff/councils/working groups, should conduct a risk assessment based on the threat, asset criticality, the program's current effectiveness, and asset vulnerability information. This risk assessment should address the likelihood of an incident and a description of the impact if the resource is not provided.

PROGRAM AND BUDGET EXECUTION REVIEW

11-6. Service components forward a copy of their antiterrorism annex to their security staff to ensure commander visibility over dedicated security resources. The following must be reported to OSD:

- Physical security equipment (blast mitigation, communications, explosive devices, barriers, intrusion detection, personal protection, other equipment/sensor, patrol/harbor boats, and high-mobility multipurpose wheeled vehicles).
- Physical security site improvement (facility modifications).
- Physical security management and planning (personnel who manage physical security programs, resources, and assets such as—but not limited to—headquarter staffs).

- Security forces/technicians (personnel and operating costs associated with protective forces used to safeguard assets, personnel, or information).
- Law enforcement (all personnel and operating costs associated with law enforcement).
- Security and investigative matters (defense criminal investigative resources, security, and any cross-discipline security functions).
- Research, Development, Test, and Evaluation (includes activities at the Defense Threat Reduction Agency and Counterterrorism Technical Support Group).

INTEGRATED PRIORITY LIST

11-7. The integrated priority list (IPL) is the principal mechanism by which combatant commanders communicate their views to the Secretary of Defense on the adequacy of the defense program. This process is designed to improve capabilities-based planning. The combatant commander's IPL focuses on a statement of key capability gaps. The IPL is expressed in terms of the capability required—not on a specific programmatic solution—and uses the framework established by the joint staff for the functional capability boards as described in Chairman of the Joint Chiefs of Staff Instruction (CJCSI) 3170.01G.

11-8. Each item on the combatant commander's IPL must perform four basic functions:

- Identify the current capability shortfall and the joint functional concept it supports.
- Cite the specific element of guidance (for example, contingency planning guidance, security cooperation guidance, or defense planning) for which the capabilities fall short.
- Describe the risks incurred by the capability shortfall, using the quadrennial defense review risk framework.
- Identify the extent to which the defense program mitigates the capability gap or shortfall.

11-9. In addition to the IPL submission, combatant commanders are also required to brief the Secretary of Defense on their IPL.

APPROPRIATION

11-10. The appropriation type must meet reference guidelines and should refer to military construction (MILCON) projects. The financial manager can help identify all fiscal and operational considerations by assisting other staff elements in validating and prioritizing requirements. This is accomplished by accurately forecasting and obtaining funds, capturing costs, and determining the correct appropriations to fund requirements. The activity/installation/unit financial manager identifies, allocates, distributes, controls, and reports fund execution for separate types of appropriations for all operations. A requirement may have more than one appropriation type—for example, if maintenance costs are associated with equipment purchase. The item to be purchased may require procurement funding and operations and maintenance funding to maintain the cost of the item in the future.

FUNDING REQUIREMENT BY FISCAL YEAR

11-11. The installation or unit resource or financial manager should be involved, along with the contracting and engineering staff, to determine the correct funding requirements. Annotate the funding requirement for each year in dollars for both the procurement of the item and the associated maintenance costs in the out years. Replacement and shelf-life issues should be considered and annotated.

COMBATANT COMMANDERS READINESS INITIATIVES FUND

11-12. If a CBT–RIF request has been submitted, annotate this and the fiscal year the request was submitted. CBT–RIF is managed by the joint staff and is used to fund the combatant commander's emergency or emergent high-priority requirements in the year of execution. If a CBT–RIF request has been submitted, indicating an emergent request, an additional request for funding should be submitted to capture the follow-on costs.

PRIORITIZING REQUIREMENTS

11-13. Once requirements are generated and documented, it is essential to analyze the justification data (threat, asset criticality, current program effectiveness, vulnerabilities, and commander's risk). Prioritize requirements focusing on the most critical and important needs first. Resources required to mitigate a major or a high-risk situation should be given priority.

11-14. Emphasis should be placed on acquiring resources to deter, detect, and defend against the terrorist threat. In addition, resource requirements necessary to adhere to DOD or Service directives, standards, instructions, or regulations should be given priority.

11-15. To assist in prioritizing resources, requirements should be placed in the following three categories of importance:

- High priority.
- Medium priority.
- Low priority.

11-16. It is recommended that activities/installations/units employ working groups and councils to assist in this effort. This ensures that commanders are aware of the wide range of risks involved. In addition, it is not necessary for each criterion to be met in a specific category for the requirement to be identified as high, medium, or low. However, a majority of the criterion should be met.

11-17. Although a requirement is identified as high/medium/low, the resource must be affordable, supportable, reduce risk, and provide a high or moderate impact on the program to achieve objectives. Once the requirements have been prioritized and categorized, an acquisition strategy should be researched, requirements submitted, and funding sources sought.

FUNDING SOURCES

11-18. A realistic and affordable budget and procurement strategy should be developed that captures all life cycle costs (manpower needs, logistics or maintenance, replacement costs). The PSO and the resource manager/financial manager or comptroller should work closely to address these requirements. The PSO is the subject matter expert responsible for articulating and justifying the requirements, and the resource manager/financial manager/comptroller is responsible for identifying accurate appropriation and funding and submitting timely funding requirement to the correct source.

11-19. The first option is to leverage the PPBES process to compete for funding. This addresses the need to fund requirements 2 years from the year of execution. It is critical to understand and use the PPBES process to obtain funding. (Information on the PPBES process can be found in Management Initiative Decision 913.) However, this process does not guarantee funding. Accurately identifying and justifying requirements is crucial.

11-20. Without proper justification, it is almost certain requirements will not be considered for funding. These requirements compete with other higher-headquarters Service responsibilities and priorities. Due to this competition for limited funding, possessing well-documented justification does not necessarily guarantee that funding will be provided. However, the unit's chances to effectively compete can be improved. In addition to properly documenting requirements, it is critical that requirements information is provided on time and in the format requested.

11-21. The second source of funding is through the CBT–RIF—its purpose being to fund emergency and emergent high-priority, combating-terrorism requirements in the year of execution. CBT–RIF provides a means for the combatant commanders to react to unforeseen requirements from changes in a terrorist threat, threat levels, and force protection doctrine/standards, as well as unanticipated requirements identified as a result of vulnerability assessments, tactical operations, and exercising antiterrorism plans. If maintenance funds for CBT–RIF projects are not programmed and provided from the parent Service, CBT–RIF can be used to fund maintenance costs for those CBT–RIF-funded items during the year of purchase and the subsequent year as a temporary measure to permit Services adequate time to program life cycle costs. The fund is not intended to subsidize ongoing projects, supplement budget shortfalls, or support routine activities—which are Service responsibilities—and does not handle the majority of force protection resource requirements.

11-22. CBT–RIF requests can only be submitted by the combatant commanders for their geographic area and area of responsibility. The combatant commanders must validate and forward CBT–RIF requests for operations and maintenance and procurement funds to the joint staff according to CBT–RIF submission, approval, and reporting procedures. Use of the core vulnerability assessment management program is required for submission of CBT–RIF requests to the joint staff.

UNFUNDED REQUIREMENTS SUBMISSION

11-23. If funding cannot be reallocated internal to the organization, UFRs are forwarded to higher headquarters.

11-24. If the component is not able to fund the requirement(s), the well-documented UFR(s) should be forwarded to the combatant commander for consideration. The combatant commander's staff is responsible for consolidating UFRs and including them in the combatant commander's IPLs submitted to OSD in October through November. OSD and the Services provide guidance during the PPBES process. The combatant commander is also required to forward consolidated component UFRs to the joint staff so that they can coordinate and make priority recommendations to the Services (November through December) in preparation for the Services' next PPBES cycle. The combatant commander's staff is also responsible for forwarding the combatant commander-approved emergent or emergency UFRs to the joint staff to compete for CBT–RIF funding.

11-25. Service security staffs shall assess and prioritize the well-documented UFRs provided by their components and recommended by the joint staff. It is important that Services receive the appropriate mandated documentation using the specified format so that they can adequately champion and defend their component's security requirements throughout the Services' corporate PPBES process. Services should ensure that funding requests are not duplicated through the two avenues (PPBES process and CBT–RIF).

11-26. OSD will review the budgets proposed by the Services to meet security objectives during the Program and Budget Execution Review (June through December). Unresolved issues and critical requirements may result in OSD program and funding direction to the Services and agencies via a Program Decision Memorandum and/or Program Budget Decision.

SECURITY OFFICER RESOURCE RESPONSIBILITIES

11-27. Once designated as a member of the security staff or as the single security point of contact, the security officer becomes the expert in the organization in generating, prioritizing, and accurately documenting security requirements. Security should be the primary duty of the designated security officer. If this is not possible, Service headquarters should consider requesting personnel to properly fill this requirement. The security officer is responsible for establishing and maintaining documentation for security resource requirements. Requirements must be continuously updated and ready for funding data requests.

Appendix A

Sample Physical Security Plan

AR 190-13 requires each installation, unit, or activity to maintain and use a detailed physical security plan. The plan should include at least special and general guard orders, access and material control, protective barriers and lighting systems, locks, and IDSs. Security plans should be used as an annex to the unit's antiterrorism plans. All physical security plans have the potential of being classified documents and must be treated accordingly. Figure A-1 is provided as a sample physical security plan.

Map Reference Copy No._____
 Issuing Headquarters
 Place of Issue
 Date of Issue

Physical Security Plan
1. Purpose. State the plan's purpose.
2. Area security. Define the areas, building, and other structures considered critical, and establish priorities for their protection.
3. Control Measures. Define and establish restrictions on access and movement into critical areas.
    a. Categorize restrictions as to personnel, materials, and vehicles.
        (1) Personnel access.
            (a) Establishment of controls pertinent to each area or structure.
                - Authority for access.
                - Criteria for access.
                    – Unit personnel.
                    – Visitors.
                    – Maintenance personnel.
                    – Contractor personnel.
                    – National Guard.
                    – Emergency response teams (police, fire, ambulance, and so forth).
            (b) Identification and control.
                - Description of the system to be used in each area. If a badge system is used, a complete description covering all aspects should be used in disseminating requirements for identification and control of personnel conducting business on the installation.
                - Application of the system.
                    – Unit personnel.
                    – Visitors to restricted areas.
                    – Visitors to administrative areas.
                    – Vendors, tradesmen, and so forth.
                    – Contractor personnel.
                    – Maintenance or support personnel.
                    – Fail-safe procedures during power outages.

Figure A-1. Sample physical security plan

(2) Material control.

    (a) Incoming.

- Requirements for admission of material and supplies.
- Search and inspection of material for possible sabotage hazards.
- Special controls on delivery of supplies or personal shipments in restricted areas.

    (b) Outgoing.

- Documentation required.
- Controls, as outlined in paragraph 3a (2a).
- Classified shipment not involving nuclear/chemical material.

    (c) Nuclear/chemical material.

- Controls on movement of warheads/chemicals on the installation.
- Controls on shipments or movement of training warheads/chemicals.
- Controls on pickup or delivery of warheads/chemicals outside the installation.

(3) Vehicle control.

    (a) Policy on search of military and privately owned vehicles.

    (b) Parking regulations.

    (c) Controls for entrance into restricted and administrative areas:

- Military vehicles.
- Privately owned vehicles.
- Emergency vehicles.
- Vehicle registration.

b. Indicate the manner in which the following security aids will be implemented on the installation:

(1) Protective barriers.

    (a) Definition.

    (b) Clear zones.

    (c) Signs.

- Types.
- Posting.

    (d) Gates.

- Location in perimeter.
- Hours of operation.
- Security requirements.
- Lock security.
- Barrier plan for each gate.

(2) Protective lighting system.

    (a) Use and control.

    (b) Inspection.

    (c) Action taken in case of commercial power failure.

    (d) Action taken in case of failure of alternate power source.

(3) Emergency lighting system.

    (a) Stationary.

    (b) Portable.

(4) Intrusion detection systems.

    (a) Security classification.

    (b) Inspection.

    (c) Use and monitoring.

    (d) Actions to be taken in case of alarm conditions.

    (e) Maintenance.

    (f) Alarm logs or registers.

Figure A-1. Sample physical security plan (continued)

        (g) Tamper-proof provisions.

        (h) Monitor-panel locations.

   (2) Communications:

        (a) Locations.

        (b) Use.

        (c) Tests.

        (d) Authentication procedures.

   (3) Security forces: General instructions that apply to all security-forces personnel (fixed and mobile). Detailed instructions, such as special orders information, should be attached as annexes. Security-force facets include:

        (a) Composition and organizations of the force.

        (b) Tour of duty.

        (c) Essential posts and routes.

        (d) Weapons and equipment.

        (e) Training.

        (f) Use of canine teams.

        (g) Method of challenging with signs and countersigns.

        (h) Alert forces:

- Composition.
- Mission.
- Weapons and equipment.
- Location.
- Deployment concept.

   (4) Contingency plans: Required actions in response to various emergency situations. Detailed plans for situations (counterterrorism, bomb threats, hostage negotiations, disaster, fire, and so forth) should be attached as annexes.

        (a) Individual actions.

        (b) Alert-force actions.

        (c) Security-force actions.

   (5) Use of air surveillance.

   (6) Coordinating instructions. Matters that require coordination with other military and civil agencies, such as—

        (a) Adjacent installations or units.

        (b) State and local agencies.

        (c) Similar host country agencies.

        (d) Federal agencies.

/signature/: commander or directorate's Signature (the document must be signed to be valid).

Figure A-1. Sample physical security plan (continued)

SUPPORT AGREEMENTS

A-1. The coordination/interaction allows for an exchange of intelligence information on security measures being used, contingency plans, and any other information to enhance local security. On an installation, the host activity shall assume responsibility for coordinating physical security efforts of all tenants, regardless of the components represented, as outlined in the support agreements and the host-activity security plan. Applicable provisions shall be included in, or be an appendix to, the support agreement. A formal agreement will contain definite assignment of physical security responsibility for the items stored. The agreement should address—

- Maximum quantities to be stored.
- Physical safeguards to be used.
- Frequency of, and responsibility for, physical inventories or reconciliations.
- Reporting of losses for investigation.
- Lock and key control.
- Unit with overall responsibility.

A-2. The physical security plan should have procedures for authorization and identification of individuals to receipt for, and physically take custody of, Army property. The purpose of such coordination is protection in depth. Authority, jurisdiction, and responsibility must be set forth in a manner that ensures protection and avoids duplication of effort.

ANNEXES TO THE PHYSICAL SECURITY PLAN

A-3. Annexes may be separated from the physical security plan for operational reasons. When separating annexes from the plan, the plan must indicate their location. Annexes to the plan should include, but are not limited to, the following (AR 190-13 provides additional information):

- **Annex A**. This annex identifies the installation threat statement resulting from the assessment completed by installation intelligence (see AR 190-13).
- **Annex B**. This annex provides a bomb-threat plan that includes, at the minimum, guidance for—
  - Controlling the operation.
  - Evacuating personnel.
  - Searching for suspicious devices.
  - Finding the bomb or suspected bomb.
  - Disposing of the bomb.
  - Reacting to detonation and damage control.
  - Controlling media inquiries.
  - Completing after action reports.
- **Annex C**. This annex addresses an installation closure plan, which identifies contingency road closings and restriction of movement within specific areas of the installation. The inclusions of this annex must be coordinated with local and state law enforcement activities.
- **Annex D**. This annex is composed of a natural-disaster plan that has been coordinated with natural-disaster plans of local jurisdictions. At the minimum, the natural-disaster plan should provide guidance for—
  - Control of the operation.
  - Continuity of operations.
  - Evacuation.
  - Communications.
  - Control of publicity.
  - An after action report.
- **Annex E**. This annex consists of the civil-disturbance plan and is formulated by the commander based on local threats. (For example, commanders of chemical facilities should anticipate the need to develop crowd-control procedures to handle antichemical demonstrations.)
- **Annex F**. This annex addresses a resource plan to meet the minimum-essential physical security needs for the installation or activity.
- **Annex G**. This annex, a communications plan, requires established communications with other federal agencies and local law-enforcement agencies to share information about possible threats. The communications plan should address all communication requirements for Annexes B through F above.
- **Annex H**. This annex is a list of designated restricted areas. Each restricted area should have been designated in writing to afford it proper protection and security.
- **Annex I**. This annex is a list of installation MEVAs.

- **Annex J**. This annex identifies a contingency plan used in situations when the commander determines that an increase in physical security measures and procedures are necessary. In most instances, it will be necessary to increase security for AA&E and other sensitive property, assets, and facilities during periods of natural disasters, national emergencies, or increased threat from terrorists or criminal elements. Other contingencies that may require an increase in physical security measures and procedures include hostage negotiations, protective services, and special-reaction teams. These provisions should be designed for early detection of an attempted intrusion, theft, or interruption of normal security conditions.
- **Annex K**. This annex identifies a work-stoppage plan. This is a requirement for conducting a physical security survey to determine the impact of a decrease in the installation's work force. A work-stoppage plan includes additional physical security considerations regarding the activity involved (such as modified or alternate staffing considerations) and the area directly surrounding critical infrastructures and critical assets. This annex should include provisions for increased access control measures if the situation warrants.

TACTICAL-ENVIRONMENT CONSIDERATIONS

A-4. In a tactical environment, the development of a physical security plan is based on METT-TC (using the operations order format and the higher headquarters order). The order may be specific about the tasks the unit will perform. Time available may be limited and the scheme of maneuver may be dictated, but the leader must evaluate the mission in terms of METT-TC to determine how Soldiers can best carry out the commander's order.

A-5. Consider each of the following factors and compare courses of action to form a base for the physical security plan. When the plan is complete, issue it as an order.

- Concepts for reconnaissance, coordination with adjacent and/or supporting units, and troop movement.
- Physical security installation configurations and facilities. Areas to consider may include ACPs, forward or deployed operational bases, staging areas, drop zones, landing zones, ranges, and training areas.

MISSION

A-6. The mission is usually the emplacement of defensive security rings to protect the populace against insurgents. The number of defensive security rings depends on the particular site and situation. The following questions must be evaluated:

- What is the mission?
- What specific and implied tasks are there to accomplish the mission?
- What is the commander's intent?

ENEMY

A-7. The commander identifies enemy/threat units operating in the area and tries to determine the type and size of the unit; the enemy's tactics, weapons, equipment, and probable collaborators; and the inhabitants' attitudes toward the threats. The following questions must be evaluated:

- What is known about the enemy?
- Where—and how strong—is the enemy?
- What weapons does the enemy have?
- What is the enemy doing?
- What can the enemy do in response to military action?
- How can we exploit the enemy's weaknesses?

TERRAIN AND WEATHER

A-8. The commander can use observation and fields of fire, avenues of approach, key terrain, obstacles, and cover and concealment (OAKOC) to plan for the physical security defensive sites. The following questions must be evaluated:

- How will the terrain and weather affect the operation?
- How fast can movement be accomplished, and how much space do the terrain and unit formations take up?
- How will the weather affect the terrain or personnel?
- Has the weather already affected the terrain?

TROOPS AND SUPPORT AVAILABLE

A-9. The commander must consider available equipment, the reaction time, reaction forces, communication assets, organization of troops, and medical support (if available). The following questions must be evaluated:

- What are the present conditions of vehicles and personnel?
- What is the status of ammunition and supplies?
- Who is best able to do a specific task?
- How much sleep have the Soldiers had in the past 24 hours?
- What other assets are available to support the mission?
- How many teams/squads are available?
- What supplies and equipment are needed?
- What fire support is available and how can it be obtained?

TIME AVAILABLE

A-10. This factor is critical since the inhabitants must be ready to respond to an insurgent attack with little or no warning. The following questions must be evaluated:

- How much time is available to conduct planning and rehearsals?
- How long will it take to reach the objective?
- How long will it take to prepare the position?
- How much time do subordinates need?
- How long will it take the enemy to reposition forces?

CIVIL CONSIDERATIONS

A-11. The commander also must consider nonbelligerent third parties (such as local civilian populations, dislocated civilians, personnel of international businesses and relief organizations, and the media). Commanders should prepare a site overlay that shows, at the minimum, the following:

- Attitude of the HN toward U.S. forces.
- Population density near the objective.
- Condition of the local civilians.
- Possible effect of refugees and dislocated civilians on the mission.

Appendix B

Selected Reachback Capabilities

Reachback is the process of obtaining products, services, and applications or forces, equipment, or material from organizations that are not forward deployed. Organizations may capitalize on and enhance their situational awareness and information superiority through reachback capabilities by accessing outside information sources. These accessible capabilities include, but are not limited to, the Center for Army Lessons Learned (CALL), Office of the Provost Marshal General, USAMPS, USACIDC, DOD Lock Program, and other federal law enforcement agencies. They also include USACE, where physical security personnel can find a variety of useful information such as protective design, security planning, and protection standards for new construction, renovation projects, and expeditionary or temporary construction projects.

CENTER FOR ARMY LESSONS LEARNED

B-1. CALL collects and analyzes data from a variety of current and historical sources, including Army operations and training events, and produces lessons for military commanders, staffs, and students. Personnel may use CALL to access articles, publications, research information, and materials by contacting the following:

- CALL Web site universal resource locator (URL): <http://call.army.mil/#>.
- CALL point of contact information is as follows:
  - Request for information, telephone (DSN) 552-9569/9533 or commercial (913) 684-9569/9533.
  - Information about CALL, telephone DSN 552-3035/2255 or commercial (913) 684-3035/2255.

OFFICE OF THE PROVOST MARSHAL GENERAL

B-2. The Office of the Provost Marshal General leads and directs policy for Army law enforcement, police intelligence, physical security, corrections and internment, criminal investigations, provost marshal activities, and other military police support as required. It supports the Army for management and execution of the Army force protection mission, including antiterrorism operations, physical security programs, and intelligence functions, and provides executive oversight of Office of the Provost Marshal General resources. Personnel may obtain information from Office of the Provost Marshal General by contacting or accessing the following:

- Office of the Provost Marshal general Web site URL: <https://www.us.army.mil/suite/page/409448>.
- Office of the Provost Marshal general point of contact information: Users may contact the following sections in the organization:
  - Army Operations Center Military Police Desk (24/7 operations), commercial (703) 693-4820.
  - Antiterrorism Section, commercial (703) 695-4912.
  - Antiterrorism Operations and Intelligence Cell, commercial (703) 697-9529.
  - Operations, commercial (703) 693-5488.
  - National Detainee Reporting Center, commercial (703) 692-7290.
  - Law Enforcement, commercial (703) 695-4210.
  - Physical Security, <https://www.us.army.mil/suite/page/441649>.
  - Corrections/Internment, commercial (703) 602-8979.

UNITED STATES ARMY MILITARY POLICE SCHOOL

B-3. USAMPS is a unique, multi-Service training facility that provides instruction to Army, Air Force, Navy, Marine, civilian, and multinational students. As the "Law Enforcement Center of Excellence," USAMPS trains military police leaders and Soldiers for full spectrum operations, prepares the Military Police Corps Regiment for the future, and fosters organizational excellence. Personnel may obtain information from USAMPS by contacting or accessing the following:

- USAMPS Web site URL: <www.us.army.mil> or <www.wood.army.mil/usamps>.
- USAMPS point of contact information is as follows:
    - Antiterrorism Branch, commercial (573) 596-2097.
    - Law Enforcement Branch, commercial (573) 596-2999.
    - Advance Investigations and Specialized Training Branch, commercial (573) 563-7787.
    - Basic Investigations Training Branch, commercial (573) 563-1083.
    - Critical Incident Peer Support, commercial (573) 563-7868.
    - Weapons of Mass Destruction Branch, commercial (573) 563 -8136.
    - Police Intelligence Operations, commercial (573) 563-5596.
    - Physical Security Branch, commercial (573) 563-5585.
    - Family Advocacy Law Enforcement Training Division, commercial (573) 563-8061.
    - Law Division, commercial (573) 563-8034.
    - Criminal Technology Training Office, commercial (573) 563-5634.
    - Law Enforcement Tactics Branch, commercial (573) 596-2091.
    - Inter-Service Nonlethal Individual Weapons Instructor Course, commercial (573) 596-2789.
    - Protective Service Training Branch, commercial (573) 596-1970.
    - Military Operations in Urban Terrain/Civil Disturbance, commercial (573) 596-2914.
    - Unarmed Self-Defense, commercial (573) 596-2631.
    - Military Police Operations, commercial (573) 596-1812.
    - Corrections, commercial (573) 596-2652.
    - Detainee Operations, commercial (573) 596-2654.
    - Directorate of Training, commercial (573) 563-8098.
    - Directorate of Plans and Operations, commercial (573) 563-7802.
    - Military Police Doctrine, commercial (573) 563-4074.
    - Individual Training Development Division, commercial (573) 563-8119.
    - Special Tactics Training Division, commercial (573) 596-0730.
    - Antiterrorism Evasive Driving Branch, commercial (573) 596-1555.
    - Personnel Proponency, Initiatives, and Integration, commercial (573) 563-8041.
    - Army Nonlethal Scalable Effects Center, commercial (573) 563-7092.
    - Lessons Learned Initiatives, commercial (573) 563-7820 or (573) 563-5665.
    - MWD Handler Course at Lackland Air Force Base, Texas, commercial (201) 671-3406.
    - MWD Supervisor/Training Course at Lackland Air Force Base, Texas, commercial (201) 671-2461.
    - Traffic Management and Accident Investigations Course at Lackland Air Force Base, Texas, commercial (201) 671-3211.
- Army Training Support Center Web site URL: <www.atsc.army.mil>.
- Army Training Information Architecture Web site URL: <www.adtdl.army.mil> or <www.train.army.mil>.
- RDL Web site URL: <www.adtdl.army.mil> or <www.train.army.mil>.

B-4. The battlefield workload analysis (BWA) worksheet is a tool used to help determine the number of military police units required to perform multiple missions. A detailed workload analysis attempts to eliminate overtasked and stressed military police personnel and ensure that adequate military police resources are applied to a mission. The BWA's interconnected formulas determine the required military police structure. There are individual tabs for combat support, MWD, law and order, and CID requirements. The BWA directly supports the military police staff running estimate and requires continuous maintenance throughout the planning, preparation, and execution of a mission in order to remain relevant as a staff planning tool. To request an automated copy or to propose comments or questions regarding the BWA, contact the military police doctrine analyst at <leon.mdottddmpdoc@conus.army.mil>.

UNITED STATES ARMY CRIMINAL INVESTIGATION COMMAND

B-5. As the Army's primary criminal investigative organization, CID is responsible for the conduct of criminal investigations in which the Army is a party of interest. The United States Army Criminal Investigation Laboratory (USACIL) provides forensic and technical services to military criminal investigators. Personnel may obtain information from USACIDC by contacting or accessing the following:

- USACIDC website URL: <www.cid.army.mil>.
- USACIDC point of contact information: Users may contact the following:
  - USACIL, commercial (404) 469-7108. USACIL provides forensic laboratory services to DOD investigative agencies and other federal law enforcement agencies. USACIL also operates as an Army school to train forensic laboratory examiners and manages the USACIDC criminalistics and visual information programs.
  - United States Army Crime Records Center (USACRC), commercial (703) 806-0431. Record checks are requested not only by USACIDC agents but also by other military and civilian law enforcement officials. USACRC is the Army's agent for Freedom of Information Act and Privacy Act requests relating to criminal investigations and military police reports. USACRC also manages the Army's polygraph programs and their support to Army installations around the world.
  - United States Protective Services Battalion (PSB), commercial (703) 806-0251/0258. PSB provides worldwide protective services and vulnerability protection to designated personnel to protect them from assassination, kidnapping, injury, or embarrassment.
  - Computer Crime Investigation Unit (CCIU), commercial (703) 805-2315/3499. CCIU deals with intrusions into the United States Army networks. CCIU works closely with military intelligence and federal law enforcement agencies to coordinate military actions, nonmilitary-affiliated offenders, and foreign intelligence services. In addition, it provides technical assistance to CID elements that are conducting computer-related investigations.

ENGINEER RESOURCES

B-6. The availability of military and civilian engineers through reachback provides support to units, improves their capabilities, and promotes mission success. Military police and engineer units often combine efforts to assure mobility and provide protection to other units and facilities. Security personnel and engineers must frequently work together to achieve mission success. Personnel may obtain information from engineer reachback sources by contacting or accessing the following:

- USAES Web site URL: <www.wood.army.mil>. USAES trains, transforms, and takes care of the Army Engineer Regiment to provide land component commanders with the joint engineer capabilities required to assure mobility of the force and achieve victory in any military operation.
- USAES points of contact are as follows:
  - Directorate of Environmental Integration, commercial (573) 563-3816.
  - Program Integration Office–Terrain Visualization Data, commercial (573) 329-1908.
  - TRADOC Capability Manager–Assured Mobility, commercial (573) 563-4081.
  - Counter Explosive Hazards Center, commercial (573) 563-4085.
  - Training Integration, commercial (573) 563-8112.
  - Improvised Explosive Device Defeat (IEDD) Training Resources: Personnel may obtain resources and training information on IEDD located at Web site URL <www.us.army.mil>.
- USACE Reachback Operations Center Web site URL and point of contact information: <https://reachback.usace.army.mil>. Telephone (251) 690-2039, (601) 634-2735/3485, or (877) 223-8322 commercial or DSN (312) 446-2735/3485. Reachback provides engineering capability that allows DOD personnel deployed worldwide to talk directly with experts in the United States when a problem in the field needs quick resolution. The USACE reachback operations center staff members respond to incoming information requests and provide detailed analyses of problems,

such as flooding potential due to dam breaches, load-carrying capacities of roads and bridges, field fortifications and force protection, and evaluation of transportation networks. Requestors/customers may send a request for information via secure or nonsecure communication network to the center. Some requests for information include, but are not limited to, environmental assessment; antiterrorism/force protection design; water and wastewater treatment infrastructure assessment; geographic information system (GIS); base camp design; access control design; system design; electrical design and analysis; route analysis and bridge military load classification; bridge and dam repair; dam breach/flood analysis; intelligence analysis; disaster relief support; and airport, port facility, railroad, and roadway design/repair.

- United States Army Corps of Engineers Protective Design Center (PDC) Web site URL: <https://pdc.usace.army.mil>. PDC is the Army's center of expertise for engineering services related to force protection and protective design. The Center provides engineering design and support services to the Army for both permanent and expedient applications and to DOD and other U.S. Government agencies to protect assets against criminal, terrorist, conventional, nuclear, and special weapons threats. The PDC has experience assisting units with vulnerability assessments and recommending mitigating measures, including vehicle barriers to achieve standoff distance and structural hardening to resist weapons effects.

- United States Army Corps of Engineers Electronic Security Center (ESC) Web site URL: <https://www.hnd.usace.army.mil/esc>. ESC is the Army Center of expertise for engineering services related to force protection and protective design, and it provides a wide range of ESS-related services to protect assets against threats and hazards. ESC provides ESS surveys, design, procurement and system installation; antiterrorism/force protection vulnerability assessments; development of criteria (such as technical and performance specifications and TMs); systems test and evaluation; and ESS training.

- Engineer Research and Development Center (ERDC) Web site URL and point of contact information: <www.erdc.usace.army.mil> and commercial (202) 761-0011. ERDC supports DOD and other federal agencies in military and civilian projects. Research projects include facilities, airfields and pavements, protective structures, sustainment engineering, environmental cleanup, topography, mapping, geospatial data, environmental impacts, flood control, navigation, compliance and conservation, and information technology.

DEPARTMENT OF DEFENSE LOCK PROGRAM

B-7. The DOD Locks, Safes, Vaults, Seals, and Containers Program is designated by the Secretary of Defense to provide management, operation, and support functions for development, testing, and procurement of locking devices, security containers, and related delay devices. Call the DOD Lock Program Technical Support Hotline, commercial (800) 290-7607, (805) 982-1212, DSN 551-1212. The Technical Support Hotline staff can help you with information on security hardware selection, requirements, specifications, national stock numbers, purchasing, training, and troubleshooting of equipment failures. Web site URL: <https://portal.navfac.navy.mil/portal/page/portal/navfac/navfac_ww_pp/navfac_nfesc_pp/locks/>

B-8. The DOD Lock Program is now providing "Open/Secured" two-sided magnetic signs to the DOD community free of charge. These signs will include the Technical Support Hotline contact information for quick reference in getting support for your security equipment. It is good practice to use these signs on containers or vault doors in order to provide a visual status of the equipment to personnel working in the area.

Appendix C

Sample Physical Security Checklist

Table C-1 is provided as a sample checklist only. Units should establish individual checklists that are based on the asset/area to be protected, acceptable risk levels, and other factors such as installation security regulations and requirements. Items marked *Critical* on this checklist will indicate a major weakness in the security plan and should be corrected immediately.

Table C-1. Sample physical security checklist

No.	Question	Critical	Adequate	Not Adequate
1.	Are primary and secondary command centers designated?			
2.	Is there a primary and secondary communications system?			
3.	Is there a physical security plan? (AR 190-13)			
4.	Is there a physical security site survey? (AR 190-13)			
5.	Is there a vulnerability assessment?			
6.	Is there a threat assessment?			
7.	Is there a criticality assessment?			
8.	Is there a risk assessment? (DA Pam 190-51)			
9.	Is the perimeter of the facility or activity defined by a barrier or fence system?			
10.	Are the fences or barriers strong and in good repair?			
11.	Are the fence and barrier heights designed so that an intruder cannot climb over them? (UFGS-32 31 13.53)			
12.	Does the fence have a top guard strung with barbed wire and angled outward and upward at a 45° angle? (UFGS-32 31 13.53)			
13.	Are there any gaps under the fence that an intruder could crawl through?			
14.	Are boxes or other items stored next to the fence or barrier, enabling the intruder to climb over it?			
15.	Is there a clear area on both sides of the fence or barrier?			
16.	Are there any unsecured overpasses or subterranean passageways near the fence or barrier?			
17.	Are openings (such as culverts, tunnels, and manholes for sewers and utility access) and sidewalk elevators (which permit access to the facility) properly secured?			

Table C-1. Sample physical security checklist

No.	Question	Critical	Adequate	Not Adequate
18.	Does any body of water (such as rivers, lakes, ponds) form a part of the installation barrier system? If so, what security measures have been taken to ensure that these barriers match or exceed the rest of the perimeter security?			
19.	Does any part of a wall or building form part of the perimeter barrier? If so, does it meet the minimum requirements for perimeter fencing?			
20.	Have shrubbery and underbrush near the perimeter fence and barriers been kept to a minimum?			
21.	Is there shrubbery or underbrush next to buildings?			
22.	Are boxes or other items stacked near or against buildings?			
23.	Are all perimeter entrances equipped with secure locking devices, and are they used when the entrance or gate is not in use? (AR 190-51)			
24.	Are access gates solid and in good condition?			
25.	Are access gates properly locked when not in use?			
26.	Are gate hinges secure and nonremovable?			
27.	Do the lock and chain used to secure gates meet DOD specifications? (UFGS-32 31 13.53)			
28.	Are the gates that are locked checked on a regular basis?			
29.	Who is responsible for the keys to the perimeter entrances? (Local SOP)			
30.	Are perimeter entrance keys signed out on a key control roster? (AR 190-51)			
31.	Are appropriate signs setting forth the provisions for entry to the installation visibly posted at all principal entrances?			
32.	Are other appropriate warning signs posted on fences and barriers as prescribed by DOD regulations?			
33.	Are clear zones maintained on both sides of the fence or barrier for large vehicles? If clear zones are not possible, what other security arrangements have been made?			
34.	Are POVs permitted to park against, or close to, the perimeter barrier or fence? (Local policy)			
35.	How often do the maintenance crews check the perimeter fencing or barriers for repair needs? (Local policy)			
36.	Do guard patrols patrol the perimeter? How often do they make their rounds? (Security SOP)			

Table C-1. Sample physical security checklist

No.	Question	Critical	Adequate	Not Adequate
37.	Are perimeter security breaches or inadequacies reported immediately and acted on, with necessary repairs made?			
38.	Is the perimeter of the facility reinforced by protective lighting? (UFC 3-530-01)			
39.	Is there adequate lighting at all ACPs to ensure proper identification of individuals, examination of credentials, and safe and efficient inspection of vehicles?			
40.	Is the lighting adequate to illuminate critical areas such as alleys, ground-level windows, and others?			
41.	Is the perimeter adequately illuminated to display intruders, but not the guard force? (UFC 3-530-01)			
42.	Are the entrances to buildings and other facilities adequately illuminated? (UFC 3-530-01)			
43.	Are the protective lighting system and the working lighting systems on the same power source line?			
44.	Is there an auxiliary power source for the protective lighting?			
45.	Has the auxiliary power source been tested?			
46.	Does the auxiliary power source automatically switch on when the main power goes off?			
47.	Is perimeter and other security lighting set to come on at dark—or must it be manually turned on?			
48.	Can the lighting system be compromised easily?			
49.	Is there a backup system for interior lighting?			
50.	Is interior daylight lighting adequate for security purposes?			
51.	Is interior night lighting adequate for security purposes?			
52.	Does interior lighting support CCTV? (UFC 3-530-01)			
53.	Are the perimeter fences and barriers augmented by IDS?			
54.	Does protective lighting cover the IDS? (UFC 3-530-01)			
55.	Is there a central control center for the IDS? (UFC 4-021-02NF)			
56.	Is there debris or other material stacked against buildings?			
57.	Are nonessential or unused windows and doors either blocked with steel mesh or bricked up?			
58.	Are windows within 14 feet of the ground covered with protective grillwork?			
59.	Are locks that secure windows situated so that they cannot be reached or opened by breaking the window?			

Table C-1. Sample physical security checklist

No.	Question	Critical	Adequate	Not Adequate
60.	Are windows near or under loading docks secured?			
61.	Are exposed roof hatches and skylights protected or secured?			
62.	Are fan openings or ventilator shafts properly secured?			
63.	Are service tunnels or sewers secured?			
64.	Are the fire exits or escapes designed so that exiting is easy but reentry is difficult?			
65.	Are fire doors linked to an alarm system—either portable or connected to a central control facility?			
66.	Are doors constructed of solid material?			
67.	Are door hinges installed on the inward side of the door?			
68.	Are hinge pins spot-welded to prevent removal?			
69.	Is each door equipped with an approved locking device?			
70.	Are doors locked when unattended or not in use?			
71.	Are the key control procedures in compliance with AR 190-51 and AR 190-11? (See the key control checklist appendix.)			

Legend:	
ACP	access control point
AR	Army regulation
CCTV	closed-circuit television
DA	Department of the Army
DOD	Department of Defense
IDS	intrusion-detection device
POV	privately owned vehicle
SOP	standing operating procedure
TM	technical manual
UFC	unified facilities criteria
UFGS	unified facilities guide specifications

Appendix D

Bomb Threats

Bomb threats are delivered either by phone, a recording, or in a letter. A threat by telephone could come from the person(s) who planted the device or a third party who has knowledge of the device's location. There are generally two reasons for reporting a bomb.

- The caller wants to minimize personal injury or property damage.
- The caller wants to create an atmosphere of panic and anxiety to disrupt the normal activities of the facility where the device is planted.

If there is one point that cannot be overemphasized, it is the value of being prepared. Developing a bomb incident plan can significantly reduce the potential for personal injury and property damage.

BOMB THREAT PLANNING

D-1. There are six steps that should be taken when planning for a bomb incident. They are—

- Develop a bomb incident plan/strategy.
- Prepare implementation procedures that are consistent with the strategy.
- Train personnel responsible for carrying out the plan.
- Implement the plan.
- Test the plan.
- Evaluate the results.

D-2. A bomb incident plan should cover the following major areas:

- Purpose and objective of the plan.
- Chain of command.
- Designated primary and secondary command centers.
- Establishment of primary and secondary means of communications.
- Major preventive, anticipatory, and response functions.
- Responsibilities assigned to particular positions or persons.
- Interfaces with outside response agencies, such as local police and fire departments.
- Equipment required.
- An approach for synchronizing elements of the plan.

D-3. The plan provides an overall framework that allows a variety of response options at the outset and during the course of the bomb incident.

D-4. A balanced plan for the management of a bomb threat should include the following proactive steps:

- Coordinate with law enforcement agencies (both federal and civilian) to learn the methods and operating locales of groups known to use bombs. Determine if your facility could be a potential target.
- Stay current with new developments in bomb construction and concealment.
- Confer with security counterparts to learn the bomb incident experiences of other organizations and agencies. Set up information-sharing agreements.
- Coordinate with bomb disposal experts to train unit personnel on recognition of bombs and the proper response to bomb incidents. Train key personnel whose duties bring them into contact with mail bombs.

- Control suspect packages entering unit facilities. Control can be done by inspecting the packages at a location that poses minimum danger to personnel and facilities in the event of an explosion.
- Maintain access control on personnel entering and leaving the facility.
- Educate unit personnel to look for and report any unknown or unauthorized visitors, individuals, or activities in the facility.
- Educate unit personnel and visitors to not leave bags, briefcases, boxes, and other packages unattended in public areas of the facility.
- Conduct periodic inspections of likely places that an IED could be hidden.
- Ensure that all physical security measures are in place and functional for the protected asset.
- Maintain a blueprint or floor plan of the facility.
- Maintain a telephone number roster of all necessary emergency and contact numbers.
- Educate personnel to look for and report unusual activities that might signal the early stage of a bombing attempt.
- Maintain a highly visible security patrol, which will be a significant deterrent.
- Maintain and follow the installation physical security plan.

D-5. Doors or access ways to such areas as boiler rooms, mail rooms, computer areas, elevator control rooms should remain locked when not in use and checked on a regular basis. Good housekeeping is also vital. Trash or dumpster areas should remain free of debris. These sites pose an easy place to hide an IED.

EVACUATION DRILLS

D-6. Evacuation and search drills should be performed periodically under the supervision of the installation or unit senior officer. The drills should be held in cooperation with local police, if possible. Personnel in adjacent buildings should be informed of drills to avoid causing unnecessary alarm.

D-7. Evacuation procedures depend on the circumstances. Prepare, publicize, and rehearse evacuation plans in advance. Address alarm systems, assembly areas, routes to assembly areas, personnel-evacuation responses, building and area clearances, and evacuation drills.

PERSONNEL EVACUATION RESPONSE

D-8. The bomb-threat alarm system should be easily distinguished from the fire alarm. When the alarm sounds, personnel should—

- Lock up or secure all classified materials.
- Conduct a quick visual search of their immediate working area.
- Open windows (wherever possible).
- Leave the building, taking only valuable personal belongings.
- Leave doors open and immediately proceed to the assembly area.

D-9. Opening the building will reduce internal damage due to blast effects. It will also somewhat mitigate the extent of debris flying out of or falling from the building should a detonation occur.

ASSEMBLY AREAS

D-10. Choose the routes to the assembly area so that personnel do not approach the IED at any time. Preselect the routes to the assembly area, but devise a system to inform personnel of the location of the suspected IED and alternate routes. Routes prevent confusion and bunching and avoid potential hazards (such as plate glass, windows, and likely locations of additional IEDs).

D-11. Assembly areas should be preselected and well known to personnel. Establish a clearly defined procedure for controlling, marshaling, and checking personnel in the assembly area. If buildings or establishments are in a public area, coordinate the assembly areas with local police. Assembly areas are selected using the following criteria:

- Locate assembly areas at least 100 meters from the likely target or building, if possible.

- Locate assembly areas in areas where there is little chance of an IED being hidden. Open spaces are best. Avoid parking areas because IEDs can be easily hidden in vehicles.
- Select alternate assembly areas to reduce the likelihood of ambush with a second IED. If possible, search the assembly area before personnel occupy the space.
- Avoid locating assembly areas near expanses of plate glass or windows. Blast effects can cause windows to be sucked outward rather than blown inward.
- Select multiple assembly areas (if possible) to reduce the concentration of key personnel. Drill and exercise personnel should go to different assembly areas to avoid developing an evacuation and emergency pattern that can be used by terrorists to attack identifiable key personnel.

BUILDING AND AREA CLEARANCE

D-12. Establish procedures to ensure that threatened buildings and areas are cleared, and prevent unauthorized personnel from reentering the building. Establish a cordon to prevent personnel from entering the danger area. Use security personnel to operate an ACP to monitor and control access to the area by authorized personnel only. Select a suitable building or area at a safe distance from the threatened area to be used as the incident command post. Consider locating a staging area near the incident command post suitable for large vehicles such as fire and rescue. Emergency response personnel should be prepared to cordon suspicious objects to a distance of at least 100 meters, and cordon suspicious vehicles to a distance of at least 200 meters.

D-13. ACPs, cordon areas, and the incident command post should remain operational until the provost marshal, security police, security forces, or local police have completed their examination or stated that the incident has been resolved.

BOMB THREAT RESPONSE

D-14. When receiving a telephonic threat, treat the call seriously. Do as many of the following suggestions as time and the caller will permit. Have more than one person listen in on the call.

- Keep caller on the line as long as possible by using a calm response to the threat.
- Ask caller to repeat the message.
- Record every word spoken by the caller.
- Ask for specific details on the device if the caller does not give them.
- Inform the caller that the building or facility is occupied and that many innocent people will be hurt or killed.
- Pay attention to background noise, which may give clues to the caller's location.
- Listen to the caller's voice, noting whether it is calm or agitated. Determine if the caller is male or female.
- Report the call to the proper chain of command or law enforcement agency as soon as possible.
- Remain available to answer questions by the chain of command.

D-15. When written threats are received, save all materials, including the envelope or container that the message came in. Unnecessary handling of the envelope should be avoided. Turn everything over to the chain of command or law enforcement personnel.

D-16. When an anonymous warning or threat is received, initiate the bomb-threat data card and follow established notification procedures. Local SOPs will determine subsequent actions. Immediate action may include a search without evacuation, the movement of personnel within the establishment, a partial evacuation, or a total evacuation. The following criteria help determine what immediate action to take:

- Factors favoring a search before the movement of personnel:
  - There is a high incidence of hoax telephone threats.
  - Effective security arrangements have been established.
  - Information in the warning is imprecise or incorrect.
  - The caller sounded intoxicated, amused, or very young.
  - The prevailing threat of terrorist activity is low.

- Factors favoring movement of personnel before searching:
    - Information in the warning is precise as to the matters of location, a description of the device, the timing, and the motive for the attack.
    - A prevailing threat of terrorist activity is high.

D-17. If the threat is perceived as real, begin the evacuation as outlined in the bomb threat plan.

SUSPECTED IMPROVISED EXPLOSIVE DEVICE SEARCH

D-18. Searches are conducted in response to a telephonic threat or a report of an unidentified object on or near premises occupied by DOD personnel. The following types of searches may be used when searching for a suspected bomb or IED:

- An occupant search is used when the threat's credibility is low. Occupants search their own areas. The search is completed quickly because occupants know their area and are most likely to notice anything unusual.
- A team search is used when the threat's credibility is high. The search is very thorough and places the minimum number of personnel at risk. Evacuate the area completely, and ensure that it remains evacuated until the search is complete. Search teams will make a slow, thorough, systematic search of the area.

D-19. The following procedures should be followed if a search for explosive devices must be conducted before qualified explosive ordnance disposal teams arrive:

- Make an audio check, listening for unusual sounds.
- Sweep the area visually up to the waist, and then sweep up to the ceiling. Do not forget the tops of cabinets and cupboards.
- Perform a thorough and systematic search in and around containers and fixtures.
- Pass search results as quickly as possible to the leader responsible for controlling the search area.
- Do not use a radio; it may detonate the explosive.

D-20. Circumstances might arise in the case of a very short warning period. In other instances, a threat of a bomb against some facilities (if true) might necessitate the evacuation of a very large area. In these circumstances, searching for the presence of an explosive device to identify its location, appearance, and possible operating characteristics may be warranted.

D-21. Personnel who have not been trained in IED search and identification techniques should not search for explosive devices. Two types of errors are very common—the false identification of objects as IEDs and the incorrect identification of IEDs as benign objects. Depending on the devices used to arm and trigger an IED, the search process could actually result in an explosion.

SEARCH ORGANIZATION

D-22. The person controlling the search should have a method of tracking and recording the search results (such as a diagram of the area). Delegate areas of responsibility to the search-team leader, who should report to the person controlling the search when each area has been cleared. Pay particular attention to entrances, toilets, corridors, stairs, unlocked closets, storage spaces, rooms and areas not checked by usual occupants, external building areas, window ledges, ventilators, courtyards, and spaces shielded from normal view.

DISCOVERY OF A SUSPECTED IMPROVISED EXPLOSIVE DEVICE

D-23. Under no circumstances will untrained personnel handle or attempt to dismantle a suspected IED; only trained explosive ordnance disposal personnel should handle the IED.

D-24. When a suspicious object has been found, report its location and general description immediately to the nearest law enforcement or supervisory person. Do not touch or move a suspicious object. Instead, perform the following steps:

- If an object appears in an area associated with a specific individual or a clearly identified area—
    - Ask the individual/occupant to describe objects they have brought to work in the past few days.

- Ask for an accounting of objects.
- Ask for a verbal description/identification of objects.
- If an object's presence remains inexplicable—
  - Evacuate buildings and surrounding areas, including the search team.
  - Ensure that evacuated areas are at least 100 meters from the suspicious object.
  - Establish a cordon and an incident command post.
  - Inform personnel at the incident command post that an object has been found.
  - Keep the person who located the object at the incident command post until questioned.
  - Avoid reentering the facility to identify an object that may or may not be an IED.

REACTING TO AN EXPLODED IMPROVISED EXPLOSIVE DEVICE

D-25. The following procedures should be taken when an explosive/IED detonates at a DOD facility:
- For explosions without casualties—
  - Maintain the cordon. Allow only authorized personnel into the explosion area.
  - Conduct a search of the area for any secondary devices, when possible, before emergency personnel enter the scene.
  - Fight any fires threatening undamaged buildings without risking personnel.
  - Report the explosion to the provost marshal, security police, security forces, or local police if they are not on the scene.
  - Report the explosion to the installation operations center even if an explosive ordnance disposal team is on its way. Provide as much detail as possible, such as the time of the explosion, the number of explosions, the color of smoke, and the speed and spread of fire.
  - Ensure that a clear passage for emergency vehicles (fire trucks, ambulances, and so forth) and corresponding personnel is maintained.
  - Refer media inquiries to the Public Affairs Office.
  - Establish a separate information center to handle inquiries from concerned friends and relatives.
- For explosions with casualties—
  - Select a small number of personnel to help search for casualties.
  - Conduct a search of the area for any secondary devices, when possible, before emergency personnel enter the scene.
  - Assign additional personnel the responsibility for maintaining the cordon to keep additional volunteers searching for casualties. Maintain the cordon until the explosive ordnance disposal team verifies no further presence of bombs/IEDs at the site and the fire marshal determines that risk of additional injury to searchers is over.
  - Prepare a casualty list and provide to the chain of command and/or Casualty Assistance Center. The Casualty Assistance Center is responsible for notification of next of kin.
  - Arrange for unaffected personnel to contact their next of kin.

D-26. Civilian management officials and subordinate military commanders continue to have important personal roles to fulfill during a bomb/IED attack on DOD personnel, facilities, and assets. Perform the following procedures when reporting an attack:
- Pass available information to the operations center.
- Avoid delaying reports due to lack of information; report what is known. Do not take risks to obtain information.
- Include the following information in the report:
  - Any warning received and how it was received.
  - Identity of the person who discovered the device.
  - How the device was discovered (casual discovery or organized search).
  - Location of the device (give as much detail as possible).
  - Time of discovery.

- Estimated length of time the device has been in its location.
- Description of the device (give as much detail as possible).
- Safety measures taken.
- Suggested routes to the scene.
- Any other pertinent information.

D-27. Perform the following procedures when providing emergency assistance to authorities:

- Ensure that the provost marshal, security police, security forces, and other emergency-response units from local police, fire and rescue, and explosive ordnance disposal teams are not impeded from reaching the incident command post. Help maintain crowd control and emergency services' access to the site.
- Evacuate through the doors and windows of buildings.
- Assist the on-scene commander by obtaining a building diagram showing detailed plans of the public-service conduits (gas, electricity, central heating, and so forth), if possible. If unavailable, a sketch can be drawn by someone with detailed knowledge of the building.
- Locate, identify, and make witnesses available to investigative agency representatives when they arrive on the scene. Witnesses include the person who discovered the device, witnessed the explosion, or possesses detailed knowledge of the building or area.

D-28. Performing the above steps will provide substantial assistance to the crisis-management team and give other personnel constructive, supportive actions to take in resolving the crisis. Care must be exercised, however, that additional explosive devices are not concealed for detonation during the midst of rescue operations. These attacks add to the physical damage and emotional devastation of bomb/IED attacks.

D-29. The use of bombs and IEDs during terrorist attacks against DOD personnel, facilities, and assets is a common occurrence. The procedures outlined in this appendix are intended to help a DOD facility respond to an attack before an explosive device detonates. The procedures are also intended to help mitigate the consequences of an attack in case efforts to find an explosive device and render it inoperable are not successful. Incurring the costs to DOD facilities and installations of detecting an explosive device and terminating a terrorist incident before the device can detonate are almost always preferable rather than exercising plans and options to respond to a detonation. Several of the security measures discussed will help reduce the likelihood of a successful bomb/IED attack against DOD assets.

D-30. Figure D-1 provides a quick reference checklist of information to record during a telephoned bomb threat incident.

Instructions: Be calm. Be courteous. Listen; do not interrupt the caller. Notify supervisor/security officer by prearranged signal while caller is on line.

Name _____   Time_____   Date_____

Bomb Facts

1. When is the bomb going to explode?
2. Where is the bomb right now?
3. What does the bomb look like?
4. What kind of bomb is it?
5. What will cause the bomb to explode?
6. Did you place the bomb?
7. Why?
8. What is your name and address?

If building is occupied, inform the caller that detonation could cause injury or death.

Did caller appear familiar with plant or building by his description of the bomb location?

Write out the message in its entirety and any other comments on a separate sheet of paper and attach to this checklist.

Sex   ☐ Male   ☐ Adult

      ☐ Female   ☐ Juvenile   Approximate age: Years _____

Origin of Call

☐ Local   ☐ Booth   ☐ Internal (from in the building). If internal, leave the line

☐ Long Distance   open for tracing the call.

Voice Characteristics		Speech		Language	
☐ Loud	☐ Soft	☐ Fast	☐ Distorted	☐ Excellent	☐ Good
☐ High pitch	☐ Deep	☐ Distinct	☐ Nasal	☐ Fair	☐ Poor
☐ Raspy	☐ Pleasant	☐ Stutter	☐ Lisp	☐ Foul	☐ Other
☐ Intoxicated	☐ Other	☐ Slurred	☐ Other _____		_____
_____		☐ Slow			

Accent	Manner		Background Noises	
☐ Local	☐ Calm	☐ Angry	☐ Factory machines	☐ Trains
☐ Not local	☐ Rational	☐ Irrational		☐ Animals
Region _____	☐ Coherent	☐ Incoherent	☐ Bedlam	☐ Quiet
☐ Foreign	☐ Deliberate	☐ Emotional	☐ Music	☐ Voices
Race _____	☐ Righteous	☐ Laughing	☐ Office machines	☐ Airplanes
			☐ Mixed	☐ Party atmosphere
			☐ Street traffic	

Action to Take Immediately After Call

Notify your supervisor/security officer as instructed. Do not discuss the incident with anyone other than as instructed by your supervisor/security officer.

Figure D-1. Sample bomb threat data card

This page intentionally left blank.

Appendix E

Key Control Register and Inventory Form

The key and lock custodian uses DA Form 5513 to ensure continuous accountability for keys of locks used to secure Army property and critical assets. The key control register is an important part of the overall security posture of a unit or activity and should be kept in a locked container when not in use. Refer to AR 190-11 for more information on using, filing, and storing the key control register and inventory form. Figure E-1, pages E-2 and E-3, shows a sample key control register and inventory form properly filled out.

KEY ISSUE AND TURN IN *(Continued)*					
KEY NUMBER	ISSUED (Date/Time)	ISSUED BY (Printed Name/Signature)	ISSUED TO (Printed Name/Signature)	TURNED IN (Date/Time)	RECEIVED BY (Printed Name/Signature)

INVENTORIES (JOINT/SEMIANNUAL)			
DATE	PRINTED NAME/SIGNATURE	DATE	PRINTED NAME/SIGNATURE
11 Jun 09	Ken Cox *Ken Cox*		

DA FORM 5513, SEP 2006

Page 2 of 2
APD PE v1.00

Figure E-1. Sample key control register and inventory

KEY CONTROL REGISTER AND INVENTORY
For use of this form see AR 190-11; the proponent agency is PMG.

UNIT/ACTIVITY	PERIOD COVERED
999th MP Co Blue Mountain Army Depot, VA 55555	FROM: 11 June 2009 TO:

KEY CONTROL NUMBER(S)
(Insert serial number or other identifying number from the key)

1. X313 Front Door, Bldg 101 (6 keys)	11.	21.	31.
2. G223 Back Door, Bldg 101 (8 keys)	12.	22.	32.
3. W987 1SG Office, Bldg 101 (3 keys)	13.	23.	33.
4. W955 CDR Office, Bldg 101 (3 keys)	14.	24.	34.
5. W968 TNG Office, Bldg 101 (3 keys)	15.	25.	35.
6. H883 Supply Rm, Bldg 101 (4 keys)	16.	26.	36.
7.	17.	27.	37.
8.	18.	28.	38.
9.	19.	29.	39.
10.	20.	30.	40.

KEY ISSUE AND TURN IN

KEY NUMBER	ISSUED (Date/Time)	ISSUED BY (Printed Name/Signature)	ISSUED TO (Printed Name/Signature)	TURNED IN (Date/Time)	RECEIVED BY (Printed Name/Signature)
1	11 Jun 09 0810	Cox, Ken *Ken Cox*	1SG Rollins, Mark *Mark Rollins*		
3	11 Jun 09 0810	Cox, Ken *Ken Cox*	1SG Rollins, Mark *Mark Rollins*		
1	11 Jun 09 0830	Cox, Ken *Ken Cox*	CPT Richter, Craig *Craig Richter*		
4	11 Jun 09 0830	Cox, Ken *Ken Cox*	CPT Richter, Craig *Craig Richter*		
6	12 Jun 09 1130	Cox, Ken *Ken Cox*	SFC Legate, Stephen *Stephen Legate*	12 Jun 09 1145	Cox, Ken *Ken Cox*

DA FORM 5513, SEP 2006

Page 1 of 2
APD PE v1.00

Figure E-1. Sample key control register and inventory (continued)

This page intentionally left blank.

Appendix F

Sample Key Control and Lock Security Checklist

Table F-1 is a sample key control and lock security checklist. Separate checklists should be developed to address the different requirements of AR 190-11 and AR 190-51. The different key systems should not be inspected together. Items marked *Critical* on this checklist indicate a major weakness in the key control program and should be corrected immediately.

Table F-1. Sample key control and lock security checklist

No.	Question	Critical	Adequate	Not Adequate
1.	Have a key custodian and an alternate custodian been assigned in writing (AR 190-11, paragraph 3-8c)?			
2.	Does the key custodian supervise and control the locks and keys to all buildings and entrances?			
3.	Is a current roster of these individuals kept in the unit (AR 190-11, paragraph 3-8)?			
4.	Is the key control register kept in a locked container (AR 190-11, paragraph 3-8a)?			
5.	Is a key control register (DA Form 5513) maintained and filled out properly according to AR 190-11, paragraph 3-8a?			
6.	Is the key depository according to AR 190-51, appendix D?			
7.	Are keys issued to authorized personnel in writing?			
8.	Are keys issued to other than installation/unit personnel?			
9.	Are the keys that are not in use tagged and stored in the depository?			
10.	Are duplicate keys stored in a high-security container? Is the key or the combination for this container also secured?			
11.	Are the key control registry and custodian files current and in order?			
12.	Are issued keys cross-referenced on the registry with the areas they secure?			
13.	Does the registry show— • Buildings or entrances that the keys secure? • Number and identification of keys issued? • Location and number of duplicate keys? • Issue and turn-in of keys? • Location of locks and keys held in reserve?			
14.	Does the key custodian hold an audit/inventory of the key holders asking to see the keys assigned to them?			
15.	Are current key control directives being followed?			

Table F-1. Sample key control and lock security checklist

No.	Question	Critical	Adequate	Not Adequate
16.	When personnel depart on leave, do they turn in their keys?			
17.	Are keys required for the maintenance and repair of IDS—including keys to the control unit door and monitor cabinet—kept separate from other operational IDS keys (AR 190-11, paragraph 3-8b)?			
18.	Are the keys accounted for when a person is transferred or resigns?			
19.	Are keys to arms storage buildings, rooms, racks, and containers maintained separately from other keys and accessible only to those individuals whose official duties require access to them (AR 190-11, paragraph 3-8)?			
20.	Are locks and combinations changed immediately upon a reported loss or theft of keys or transfer or resignation of personnel?			
21.	Are locks changed or rotated at least annually, regardless of transfers or known violations of key security?			
22.	Are master keys used? *			
23.	Are current records kept of combinations to safes and the dates when these combinations are changed?			
24.	Are these records adequately protected?			
25.	Are key holders ever allowed to duplicate keys? *			
26.	Are requests for duplicate keys handled according to AR 190-51?			
27.	Are padlocks and their keys inventoried by serial number semiannually (AR 190-11, paragraph 3-8e)?			
28.	Are locks on inactive gates and storage facilities under seal? Do key control personnel check seals regularly?			
29.	Are measures in effect to prevent the unauthorized removal of locks on open cabinets, gates, or buildings?			
30.	Are losses of thefts of keys and padlocks promptly reported and investigated by key custodians?			
31.	After new construction of buildings, did the contractor turn over all the keys? Were the locks changed shortly after the building was turned over for government use?			
32.	If removable-core locks are in use, are unused cores and core change keys given maximum security against theft, loss, or compromise?			
33.	Are combination lock, key, and key registries safeguarded separately (such as in a separate container) from keys, locks, cores, and other security hardware?			
34.	Are combinations to locks on vault doors or GSA-approved Class 5 or Class 6 security containers changed annually or upon change of custodian or armorer (AR 190-11, paragraph 3-8g)?			

Table F-1. Sample key control and lock security checklist

No.	Question	Critical	Adequate	Not Adequate
35.	Do all locks meet DOD standards as outlined in Federal Specifications? (FS FF-L-2740A)			
36.	Have manufacturers' serial numbers on combination locks and padlocks been properly accounted for, according to DOD and Army regulations?			
37.	When was the last key/lock visual audit made?			

* If the answer to this question is YES, key security has been violated, according to AR 190-51.

Legend:
AR   Army regulation
DA   Department of the Army
DOD   Department of Defense
GSA   United States General Services Administration
IDS   intrusion detection system

This page intentionally left blank.

Glossary

AA&E	arms, ammunition, and explosives
AC	alternating current
ACP	access control point
ACS	access control system
APOD	aerial port of debarkation
APOE	aerial port of embarkation
AR	Army regulation
ARNG	Army National Guard
ARNGUS	Army National Guard of the United States
ATTN	attention
ATTP	Army tactics, techniques, and procedures
ASTM	American Society for Testing and Materials
BMS	balanced magnetic switch
BWA	battlefield workload analysis
CAC	common access card
CALL	Center for Army Lessons Learned
CBT–RIF	Combating Terrorism Readiness Initiatives Fund
CCIU	Computer Crime Investigation Unit
CCTV	closed-circuit television
CID	Criminal Investigation Division
CJCSI	Chairman of the Joint Chiefs of Staff Instruction
CONUS	continental United States
DA	Department of the Army
DC	District of Columbia
DOD	Department of Defense
DSN	Defense Switched Network
DTM	data-transmission media
DVR	digital video recorder
ERDC	Engineer Research and Development Center
ESC	United States Army Corps of Engineers Electronic Security center
ESS	electronic security system
FAA	Federal Aviation Agency
FIPS	Federal Information Processing Standards
FM	field manual
FPCON	force protection condition
G-7	assistant chief of staff, information engagement
GIS	geographic information system

GSA	United States General Services Administration
GTA	graphic training aid
HAZMAT	hazardous material
HN	host nation
HSPD	Homeland Security Presidential Directive
ICIDS	integrated commercial intrusion detection system
IDN	initial distribution number
IDS	intrusion detection system
IED	improvised explosive device
IEDD	improvised explosive device defeat
IESNA	Illuminating Engineering Society of North America
IPL	integrated priority list
IR	infrared
ITO	installation transportation officer
JP	joint publication
LED	light-emitting diode
MA	milliamperes
MANSCEN	United States Army Maneuver Support Center
METT-TC	mission, enemy, terrain and weather, troops and support available, time available, and civilian considerations
MEVA	mission-essential or vulnerable area
MILCON	military construction
MIL-HDBK	military handbook
MSCoE	United States Army Maneuver Support Center of Excellence
MWD	military working dog
OAKOC	observation and fields of fire, avenues of approach, key terrain, obstacles, and cover and concealment
OCONUS	outside the continental United States
OPCON	operational control
OSD	Office of the Secretary of Defense
PACOM	United States Pacific Command
pam	pamphlet
PDC	United States Army Corps of Engineers Protective Design Center
PIR	passive infrared
POE	port of embarkation
POL	petroleum, oil, and lubricants
PPBES	planning, programming, budgeting, and execution system
PSB	Protective Services Battalion
PSO	physical security officer
RAM	random antiterrorism measure
R.C.M.	Rules for Courts-Martial
RF	radio frequency

ROE	rules of engagement
S-3	operations staff officer
S-4	logistics staff officer
SDDC	Surface Deployment And Distribution Command
SJA	Staff Judge Advocate
SMS (CM)	United States Army Security Management System (Countermeasures)
SOP	standing operating procedure
SPOD	seaport of debarkation
SPOE	seaport of embarkation
SRT	special reaction team
TC	training circular
TM	technical manual
TRADOC	United States Army Training and Doctrine Command
UCMJ	Uniform Code of Military Justice
UFC	unified facilities criteria
UFGS	unified facilities guide specifications
UFR	unfunded requirement
URL	universal resource locator
U.S.	United States
USACE	United States Army Corps of Engineers
USACIDC	United States Army Criminal Investigation Command
USACIL	United States Army Criminal Investigation Laboratory
USACRC	United States Army Crime Records Center
USAMPS	United States Army Military Police School
USAR	United States Army Reserves
U.S.C.	United States Code

SECTION II – TERMS

*access control point

A corridor at the installation entrance through which all vehicles and pedestrians must pass when entering or exiting the installation.

*physical security

That part of the Army security system, based on threat analysis, concerned with procedures and physical measures designed to safeguard personnel, property, and operations; to prevent unauthorized access to equipment, facilities, materiel, and information; and to protect against espionage, terrorism, sabotage, damage, misuse, and theft.

*physical security inspection

A formal, recorded assessment of the physical protective measures and security procedures that are implemented to protect unit and activity assets.

*physical security survey

A formal recorded assessment of an installation's overall physical security program, including electronic security measures.

protection

The preservation of the effectiveness and survivability of mission-related military and nonmilitary personnel, equipment, facilities, information, and infrastructure deployed or located within or outside the boundaries of a given operational area (FM 3-37).

*restricted area

Any area to which entry is subject to special restrictions or control for security reasons or to safeguard property or material.

*security procedural measures

Physical security measures to counter risk factors that will periodically change over a period of time— such as criminal, terrorist, and hostile threats. The procedures can usually be changed in a short time and involve manpower.

References

SOURCES USED

These are the sources quoted or paraphrased in this publication.

ARMY PUBLICATIONS

AR 1-1. *Planning, Programming, Budgeting, and Execution System.* 30 January 1994.

AR 50-5. *Nuclear Surety.* 1 August 2000.

AR 50-6. *Nuclear and Chemical Weapons and Materiel Chemical Surety.* 28 July 2008.

AR 190-11. *Physical Security of Arms, Ammunition, and Explosives.* 15 November 2006.

AR 190-12. *Military Working Dog Program.* 4 June 2007.

AR 190-13. *The Army Physical Security Program.* 30 September 1993.

AR 190-14. *Carrying of Firearms and Use of Force for Law Enforcement and Security Duties.* 12 March 1993.

AR 190-16. *Physical Security.* 31 May 1991.

AR 190-17. *Biological Select Agents and Toxins Security Program.* 3 September 2009.

AR 190-30. *Military Police Investigations.* 1 November 2005.

AR 190-48. *Protection of Federal Witnesses on Active Duty Installations.* 3 March 1976.

AR 190-51. *Security of Unclassified Army Property (Sensitive and Nonsensitive).* 30 September 1993.

AR 190-54. *Security of Nuclear Reactors and Special Nuclear Materials.* 19 June 2006.

AR 190-56. *The Army Civilian Police and Security Guard Program.* 15 October 2009.

AR 190-58. *Personal Security.* 22 March 1989.

AR 190-59. *Chemical Agent Security Program.* 11 September 2006.

AR 195-2. *Criminal Investigation Activities.* 15 May 2009.

AR 380-5. *Department of the Army Information Security Program.* 29 September 2000.

AR 405-20. *Federal Legislative Jurisdiction.* 21 February 1974.

AR 530-1. *Operations Security (OPSEC).* 19 April 2007.

AR 600-20. *Army Command Policy.* 18 April 2008.

FM 1-02. *Operational Terms and Graphics.* 21 September 2004.

FM 3-13. *Information Operations: Doctrine, Tactics, Techniques, and Procedures.* 28 November 2003.

FM 3-19.11. *Military Police Special-Reaction Teams.* 13 May 2005.

FM 3-19.15. *Civil Disturbance Operations.* 18 April 2005.

FM 3-19.17. *Military Working Dogs.* 6 July 2005.

FM 3-19.50. *Police Intelligence Operations.* 21 July 2006.

FM 3-34. *Engineer Operations.* 2 April 2009.

FM 3-37. *Protection.* 30 September 2009.

FM 3-90. *Tactics.* 4 July 2001.

FM 3-100.21. *Contractors on the Battlefield.* 3 January 2003.

FM 5-19. *Composite Risk Management.* 21 August 2006.

FM 5-34. *Engineer Field Data.* 19 July 2005.

FM 5-103. *Survivability.* 10 June 1985.

FM 7-15. *The Army Universal Task List.* 27 February 2009.

FM 19-10. *The Military Police Law and Order Operations.* 30 September 1987.

TC 19-210. *Access Control Handbook.* 4 October 2004.

TM 5-6350-275-10. *Operator's Manual for Integrated Commercial Intrusion Detection System (ICIDS).* 31 May 1994.

TM 5-811-1. *Electric Power Supply and Distribution.* 28 February 1995.

JOINT AND DEPARTMENT OF DEFENSE PUBLICATIONS

CJCSI 3170.01G. *Joint Capabilities Integration and Development System.* 1 March 2009.

DOD O-2000.12-H. *DOD Antiterrorism Handbook.* 1 February 2004.

DOD 5100.76-M. *Physical Security of Sensitive Conventional Arms, Ammunition, and Explosives.* 12 August 2000.

DOD 5200.08-R. *Physical Security Program.* 9 April 2007.

DODI 1325.06. *Guidelines for Handling Dissident and Protest Activities Among Members of the Armed Forces.* 27 November 2009.

DODI 2000.16. *DOD Antiterrorism (AT) Standards.* 2 October 2006.

JP 3-10. *Joint Security Operations in Theater.* 3 February 2010.

OTHER PUBLICATIONS

Army Access Control Points Standard Definitive Design and Criteria. USACE Protective Design Center. 26 May 2009. Available online at <https://pdc.usace.army.mil/library/drawings/acp>.

ASTM F 2656-07, *Standard Test Method for Vehicle Crash Testing of Perimeter Barriers.* 1 August 2007.

CIDR 195-1. *Criminal Investigation Operational Procedures.* 22 March 2010.

FF-L-2740A. *Locks, Combination.* 25 May 2001. Available online at < https://assist.daps.dla.mil/quicksearch/quicksearch_query.cfm>.

FIPS 201-1. *Personal Identity Verification (PIV) of Federal Employees and Contractors.* March 2006. Available online at < http://csrc.nist.gov/publications/fips/fips201-1/FIPS-201-1-chng1.pdf>.

GTA 90-01-011. *Joint Forward Operations Base (JFOB) Survivability and Protective Construction Handbook.* 1 October 2009.

HSPD-12. *Policy for a Common Identification Standard for Federal Employees and Contractors.* 27 August 2004. Available online at < http://www.dhs.gov/xabout/laws/gc_1217616624097.shtm>.

Management Initiative Decision 913. "Implementation of a 2-Year Planning, Programming, Budgeting, and Execution Process." May 22, 2003. Available onlne at < http://asafm.army.mil/Documents/OfficeDocuments/CostEconomics/perfmgt/mid//mid913.pdf>.

MIL-HDBK-1013/10. *Design Guidelines for Security Fencing, Gates, Barriers, and Guard Facilities.* 14 May 1993.

Office of the Provost Marshal General. *MP Policy Division Physical Security Branch.* Available online at < http://www.us.army.mil/suite/page/441649> (accessed 12 August 2010).

R.C.M. 302. "Apprehension." *Manual for Courts-Martial United States.* 2008 edition. Available online at < http://www.jag.navy.mil/documents/mcm2008.pdf>.

RR-F-191/4. *Fencing, Wire and Post, Metal (Chain-Link Fence Accessories).* 14 May 1990. Available online at < https://assist.daps.dla.mil/quicksearch/basic_profile.cfm?ident_number=51270>.

SDDCTEA Pam 55-15. *Traffic and Safety Engineering for Better Entry Control Facilities.* 2009. Available online at < http://www.tea.army.mil/pubs/nr/dod/pmd/PAM_55-15_2009.pdf>.

SF 700. *Security Container Information.*

18 U.S.C. Sec. 1382. *Crimes and Criminal Procedure.* 1 February 2010.

UCMJ, Article 7. "Apprehension." U.S. Code, 10 USC Sec. 807.

UFC 3-530-01. *Design: Interior and Exterior Lighting and Controls.* 22 August 2006. Available online at < http://www.wbdg.org/ccb/DOD/UFC/ufc_3_530_01.pdf>.

UFC 4-010-01. *DOD Minimum Antiterrorism Standards for Buildings.* 8 October 2003. Available online at < http://www.wbdg.org/ccb/DOD/UFC/ufc_4_010_01.pdf>.

UFC 4-010-02. *DOD Minimum Antiterrorism Standoff Distances for Buildings.* 8 October 2003. Available online at < http://www.wbdg.org/ccb/DOD/UFC/ufc_4_010_02.pdf>.

UFC 4-020-01A. *DOD Security Engineering Facilities Planning Manual.* 11 September 2008. Available online at < http://www.wbdg.org/ccb/DOD/UFC/ufc_4_020_01.pdf>.

UFC 4-020-04A. *Electronic Security Systems: Security Engineering.* 1 March 2005.Available online at < http://www.wbdg.org/ccb/DOD/UFC/ufc_4_020_04a.pdf>.

UFC 4-021-02NF. *Security Engineering: Electronic Security Systems.* 27 September 2006. Available online at < http://www.wbdg.org/ccb/DOD/UFC/ufc_4_021_02nf.pdf>.

UFC 4-022-01. *Security Engineering: Entry Control Facilities/Access Control Points.* 25 May 2005. Available online at < http://www.wbdg.org/ccb/DOD/UFC/ufc_4_022_01.pdf >.

UFC 4-022-02. *Selection and Application of Vehicle Barriers.* 8 June 2009. Available online at < http://www.wbdg.org/ccb/DOD/UFC/ufc_4_022_02.pdf>.

UFGS 13720A. *Electronic Security System.* October 2007.

UFGS 28 23 23.00 10. *Closed Circuit Television Systems.* April 2006. Available online at < http://www.wbdg.org/ccb/DOD/UFGS/UFGS%2028%2023%2023.00%2010.pdf>.

UFGS 32 31 13.53. *High-Security Chain Link Fences and Gates.* April 2008. Available online at < http://www.wbdg.org/ccb/DOD/UFGS/UFGS%2032%2031%2013.53.pdf>.

UFGS 34 71 13.19. *Active Vehicle Barriers.* April 2008. Available online at < http://www.wbdg.org/ccb/DOD/UFGS/UFGS%2034%2071%2013.19.pdf>.

DOCUMENTS NEEDED

These documents must be available to the intended users of this publication.

ARMY PUBLICATIONS

DA Form 2028. *Recommended Changes to Publications and Blank Forms.*

DA Form 2806-R. *Physical Security Survey Report (LRA).*

DA Form 2806-1-R. *Physical Security Inspection Report (LRA).*

DA Form 4261 and 4261-1. *Physical Security Inspector Identification Card.*

DA Form 5513. *Key Control Register and Inventory.*

RELATED PUBLICATIONS

These sources contain relevant supplemental information.

ARMY PUBLICATIONS

AR 190-5. *Motor Vehicle Traffic Supervision.* 22 May 2006.

AR 190-6. *Obtaining Information From Financial Institutions.* 9 February 2006.

AR 190-8. *Enemy Prisoners of War, Retained Personnel, Civilian Internees and Other Detainees.* 1 October 1997.

AR 190-9. *Absentee Deserter Apprehension Program and Surrender of Military Personnel to Civilian Law Enforcement Agencies.* 18 January 2007.

AR 190-24. *Armed Forces Disciplinary Control Boards and Off-Installation Liaison and Operations.* 27 July 2006.

AR 190-45. *Law Enforcement Reporting.* 30 March 2007.

AR 190-47. *The Army Corrections System.* 15 June 2006.

AR 190-53. *Interception of Wire and Oral Communications for Law Enforcement Purposes.* 3 November 1986.

AR 190-55. *U.S. Army Corrections System: Procedures for Military Executions*. 23 July 2010.

AR 385-10. *The Army Safety Program*. 23 August 2007.

AR 525-13. *Antiterrorism*. 11 September 2008.

FM 3-0. *Operations*. 27 February 2008.

FM 3-39. *Military Police Operations*. 16 February 2010.

DA Pam 190-12. *Military Working Dog Program*. 30 September 1993.

DEPARTMENT OF DEFENSE PUBLICATIONS

DODI 3224.3. *Physical Security Equipment (PSE) Research, Development, Test, and Evaluation (RDT&E)*. 1 October 2007.

DODI 5200.08. *Security of DOD Installations and Resources and the DOD Physical Security Review Board*. 10 December 2005.

DOD 5205.02-M. *DOD Operations Security (OPSEC) Program Manual*. 3 November 2008.

READINGS RECOMMENDED

Rea, Mark Stanley (Ed.). The IESNA Lighting Handbook: Reference and Application, 9th edition. New York: Illuminating Engineering Society of North America, 2000.

Index

www.ingramcontent.com/pod-product-compliance
Lightning Source LLC
Chambersburg PA
CBHW081153270326
41930CB00014B/3143